MORE FREAKY FACTS
about
NATURAL DISASTERS

MORE FREAKY FACTS
about
NATURAL DISASTERS

Kathleen Duey
and
Mary Barnes

Aladdin Paperbacks
New York London Toronto Sydney Singapore

First Aladdin Paperbacks edition July 2001

Copyright © 2001 by Kathleen Duey and Mary Barnes

Aladdin Paperbacks
An imprint of Simon & Schuster
Children's Publishing Division
1230 Avenue of the Americas
New York, NY 10020

Designed by Steve Scott
The text for this book was set in bembo.

Printed and bound in the United States of America

10 9 8 7 6 5 4 3 2 1

Library of Congress Cataloging-in-Publication Data is available.
ISBN: 0-689-82819-5

chapter one

VOLCANOES

imagine this . . .

Almost every morning of your life you have gotten out of bed and gone straight into the kitchen. It's your mother's favorite room, and her copper and iron pots hang on bright yellow walls. Eating breakfast, you always look out the picture window at your backyard, then, beyond it, at the mountain that is as familiar to you as your mother's face. Usually the gray blue of its granite ledges blurs in the early-morning mist and blends with the deep green of the pines that forest its lower slopes.

This morning is different. There is a thin trail of what looks like black smoke rising from the top of your mountain. Just as your mother comes in from feeding the dogs the earth vibrates. You hear a low rumble, like thunder but different. The back door slams open and your father comes in, shouting something about a warning on the radio. Abruptly you recall that for years scientists have been saying the volcano would erupt "someday." Maybe, you hear yourself thinking over the thudding of your pulse, today is someday.

In two or three frantic minutes you are jammed between your parents in the front seat of your father's pickup truck. He drives recklessly fast down the long dirt road that leads back to the highway. You are nearly at the blacktop when your ears are assaulted by a sound you will never be able to describe. The trees sway and an invisible fist seems to strike the truck, shoving it off the road. The day seems to become night, and you feel yourself falling toward the darkness.

When you regain consciousness, your father is bending over you. His face is tense with worry and fear. You can hear your mother crying. The sky is a weird color of gray. There is a strange smell in the air too. You get up slowly, trying to focus on your father's questions as he asks you if you are in pain, if you are dizzy. You look back toward the mountain in the distance. It has changed shape, and the trickle of smoke has become a billowing, rising cloud that reminds you of pictures you have seen of nuclear explosions.

After a few minutes you all get back into the truck, using the driver's door. The passenger door was smashed against the tree that stopped the truck from rolling—it will not open. Grinding gears, your father manages to get the truck back on the dirt road and guns the engine into a roar. Then, half a mile later, rounding the bend, you can see the highway; it is packed with cars. Your father brakes, slewing the truck to one side, then edges forward, waiting to join the lines of cars. No one slows to let him in.

"They said it was going to erupt in the next forty or fifty years, didn't they?" your mother says quietly, tears in her eyes. She blinks to clear her vision, then sighs. "I wonder if Pete Newsom got out."

Pete Newsom. You feel guilty for not thinking about your elderly neighbor across the valley on your own, and you say a silent prayer that the friendly old man is still alive.

"I wonder if the house is still there," your father says quietly.

For the first time you remember the dogs, and you bite your lip. Someone should have remembered them—you should have. They could have ridden in the back of the truck. But why hadn't they been on the back porch? They were always on the back porch. You turn to look back at the mountain you have known all your life, then look forward again when the truck lurches. Your father has put the truck in gear to crawl forward, forcing an older man in a white Cadillac to slow enough for the truck to swing into line.

Glancing backward again, you see a flash of fiery red through the smoke, then a bolt of what looks like lightning. Why would a cloud of ash and dust and smoke have lightning in it?

None of this seems real, but it is. A volcano has changed your life forever. Your father pulls in a deep breath

*as your mother strikes the dashboard with a closed fist,
then begins to cry again.*

Lava is *liquid* rock. This is well known, but that
doesn't make it any less freaky.

In ancient times people feared and worshiped
volcanoes. Powerful and destructive eruptions *still*
fascinate people. The third week of August is
National Hot Lava Week.

Some volcanoes are active (erupting), some
active but dormant (not erupting currently), and
some extinct (no longer active). About 550 eruptions have been recorded on Earth's surface; many
more have occurred unobserved on the ocean floor.

Lava is red-orange hot when it pours or blasts
out of a volcanic vent; as it cools it darkens to red,
gray, black, or some other dark color, and whatever
dissolved gases it contains are freed.

Very hot, gas-rich lava is fluid and flows like hot
tar. Cooler, gas-poor lava flows like thick honey, sometimes in pasty, blocky masses. Sometimes lava oozes

gently from the ground; other times it forms violently spectacular fire fountains. Lava rivers can cover miles of land—burning, crushing, or burying everything.

Lava flowing onto (or beneath) ice and snow can cause a destructive flood or a lahar, a mixture of water, rock, sand, and mud that flows violently away from a volcano. A lahar can rush fifty miles down a valley at twenty to forty miles per hour. It sometimes looks like a river of wet concrete and can topple boulders, trees, houses, and bridges. Once lahars lose force, they bury everything in gluey, destructive mud.

Some of the finest volcanic ash particles are thrown so far into the stratosphere that high-level winds carry them around the world many times before they finally fall back to Earth.

In 1815 the Indonesian volcano Tambora erupted, filling the upper atmosphere with dust and ash. The following year, 1816, was called the Year Without a Summer. Snow fell over New England in June. That summer was especially dreary for Mary Wollstonecraft, vacationing in Switzerland with her fiancé and friends. Stuck indoors in the gloomy weather, they wrote scary stories for fun.

The woman would become known as Mary Shelley, and her story was *Frankenstein*.

There are two kinds of lava flows; both have Hawaiian names. *Aa* (pronounced "ah-ah") flows carry sharp, angular chunks of lava known as scoria. Even cooled, the sharp, jutting rocks are dangerous and painful to cross. *Pahoehoe* (pa-hoy-hoy) flows form a smooth, pliable skin that traps gas, keeping the lava beneath hot and mobile. The hidden current of hot lava flowing inside sometimes wrinkles the cooled skin into ropelike coils.

Scientists working close to volcanoes wear helmets and fireproof "anti-volcanic-bomb" shoulder pads. In the slang used by people who study volcanoes (vulcanologists), a "bomb" is a rounded chunk of magma (molten rock beneath Earth's surface) that explodes upward from a volcanic vent, then falls. "Blocks" are more-angular rock fragments. Both are deadly—and can be house-size or as small as tennis balls. Liquid bombs plop to the ground; denser, more solid bombs and blocks thud or shatter as they hit. Many have oddly twisted tails; the lava cools and hardens as it spins through the air.

✯   ✯   ✯   ✯   ✯   ✯

The volcanic crater of Kawah Idjen holds a lake filled with water so acid it would burn through human flesh in minutes. The acidity is caused by volcanic gases dissolving in the water.

Pyroclastic flows are made of volcanic gases and ash—some reach more than 600°F. Ash and gases can flow fast—from 60 to 450 miles per hour. Most of the worst volcanic disasters (Pompeii and Saint-Pierre) have been caused by pyroclastic flows, not lava.

Indonesia's thirteen-thousand-plus islands hold the incredible world record of 130 active volcanoes. Mount Merapi, in Java, is the most active and the most deadly; it erupted most recently in 1998. People have died in at least twelve of its eruptions.

On February 24, 2000, Mayon Volcano, 190 miles southeast of Manila in the Philippines, exploded in fourteen separate eruptions, launching burning rock six miles into the sky and forming 1,650°F torrents that roared downhill at fifty miles per hour.

Volcanic gases are deadly poison. Carbon dioxide is hard to detect. Hydrogen sulfide smells like rotten eggs. Hydrogen chloride and sulfur dioxide sting the eyes and throat. Hydrogen fluoride is strong enough to etch glass. All can and do kill.

More than 80 percent of the earth's surface—above and below sea level—was formed by volcanic activity. Volcanic gases formed Earth's earliest oceans and atmosphere—ingredients vital to life.

Kilauea, on the Big Island of Hawaii, hasn't stopped erupting since 1983. By May 1990 its lava had flowed twenty miles over the land, a fiery river that obliterated the town of Kalapana.

Kilauea pumps hundreds of tons of lava a day through underground tubes and running magma rivers. When it hits the ocean, clouds of steam four to five stories high billow upward.

Volcanic islands often have black sand beaches. When lava hits the sea, the molten rock shatters into tiny, glassy particles.

In August 1986, in Lake Nyos in Cameroon, West Africa, a volcano released a cloud of noxious fumes. Flowing downhill, the gases killed 1,700 people in the villages below the lake.

✳ ✳ ✳ ✳ ✳ ✳

Scientists on the research ship *Melville* discovered the world's largest known cluster of active volcanoes deep in the South Pacific, six hundred miles northwest of Easter Island. There are, incredibly, 1,133 seamounts (undersea volcanic mountains) and volcanic cones in an area the size of New York State. Some are nearly 7,000 feet high—still 2,500 to 5,000 feet *below* the ocean's surface.

The tiny lava fragments in ash clouds rub against one another, creating static electricity, which is released in lightning that flashes through the ash clouds like a weird, dry thunderstorm.

Rock stars, jet-setters, and vacationers enjoyed the tropical Caribbean island paradise of Montserrat until its Soufrière Hills volcano—asleep for 350 years—roared back to life in July 1995. The eruption and pyroclastic flow destroyed seven villages and scorched the long-abandoned capital. Twenty people died, and the southern two-thirds of the island was destroyed. Eight thousand of the island's twelve thousand residents evacuated. Local home owners Paul McCartney, Elton John, Eric Clapton, Sting, Mark Knopfler, and others staged a benefit concert.

✕   ✕   ✕   ✕   ✕   ✕

Earth's oceans widen about an inch a year as the tectonic plates forming Earth's surface separate, opening fissures (cracks). Undersea, lava quietly fills the gaps, forming new ocean crust. On land, fissures can be dangerous. In 1783 a fissure in Iceland seeped 3.1 cubic miles of lava in eight months. The dust and gas killed 75 percent of Iceland's animals. Since Icelanders were hunters, ten thousand people died in the volcano-caused famine.

Pumice stone forms from lava containing dissolved gases that bubble and fizz in lake water or seawater. If the pumice is frothy enough, it forms stone light enough to float.

In Japan warm volcanic sand baths are believed to cure many illnesses.

In 1789 Benjamin Franklin thought ash from a volcanic eruption in Iceland had blocked sunlight and caused a harsh winter in America.

During the Middle Ages, whenever Mount Vesuvius erupted, terrified people would parade an image of their patron saint, Januarius, through the streets. Scientists realized these parades, dutifully noted in church records, could help them date eruptions.

Before 1977 scientists thought life couldn't exist without sunlight. Then they discovered undersea black smokers, where volcanic hot springs pump black, acidic mineral water through the gaps between the constantly separating tectonic plates. These nasty, toxic waters contain arsenic and cadmium and are hot enough to melt lead. But in these poisonous, sunless waters thrive giant clams, long-necked barnacles, and bizarre five-foot-long tube worms with bloodred gills fanning out from a bone-white body. Scientists must now consider the possibility of life on scalding Mars or frozen Europa, an ice-covered moon orbiting Jupiter.

The minerals spewing out of a black smoker form chimneylike formations sometimes several stories high. In 1999 scientists used a remote-controlled chain-saw device to cut four black smokers out of the ocean bed, then hauled them to the surface, with tube worms still clinging to them. The weird chimneys had been raised through a mile and a half of cold ocean, but they heated the water to near boiling as they broke the surface!

When hot lava hits trees, they often catch fire and burn to ashes. But sometimes the tree sap turns to steam that cools the lava enough to form a hard coating over the trees. The coating hardens the stone into a tree-shaped mold. In Oregon six thousand years ago a lava flow converted a pine forest into stone tree molds that stood high above the lava surface. The wood beneath the hardened lava rotted away completely over time, leaving hollow molds of stone. Visitors to Newberry National Volcanic Monument can see this Lava Cast Forest.

The Trail of Two Forests area in Mount Saint Helens National Volcanic Monument is a two-thousand-year-old formation of tree molds surrounded by living trees—the regrowth of the forest destroyed by heat and lava long ago. Here the deep lava flow solidified around the trees instead of flowing away. Visitors can walk across the old lava bed and look down into these tree-size holes in the rock. Some are straight, others slanted if the tree was leaning or half fallen; edges often show textured imprints of bark. Some of the holes connect.

Adventurous tourists can explore the 3-D tunnel-maze.

Lava can cool on the surface and form a solid "skin" while hot lava flows beneath. This crusted skin can get to one hundred feet thick! When the lava flow stops, the tubes drain out—the hardened shell of cooled lava becomes a huge, eerie tunnel of stone.

Lava River Cave, formed thousands of years ago, was discovered about one hundred years ago when a hunter came across a place where the tunnel had caved in. It's more than a mile long, and the ceiling reaches fifty-eight feet in height. Hot lava dripping off the ceiling formed weird icicle-shaped lava stalactites; below them the cooling drips hardened into stalagmites on the floor of the lava tunnel.

A common cause of death from volcanoes is an unexpected one: starvation. Climate changes caused by reduced sunlight can make crops fail. The gases, ash, and lava from volcanoes damage farmland, and famine can follow. Tambora's 1815 eruption claimed an estimated 92,000 lives; almost 80,000 died of starvation.

✗   ✗   ✗   ✗   ✗   ✗

In June 1997 a mushroom cloud of smoke and ash rose above 17,890-foot-high Popocatepetl, a volcano about thirty-three miles southeast of Mexico City. Troops tried to evacuate thirty nearby villages, but people refused to leave, afraid bandits would plunder their possessions. They stayed; the volcano didn't erupt.

Lava can sometimes be stopped. In 1996 the Italian army detonated fifteen thousand pounds of explosives to block a Mount Etna lava tunnel threatening villages below. They worked within ten feet of the 1,800°F molten rock to build earthen walls. It worked.

Scientists studying millions of years of climate changes have noticed that during ice ages there's less volcanic activity. The weight of ice and lake water might cause stress changes in the earth's crust. Water underground, near volcanic magma, might also suppress eruptions.

Vulcanologist Thor Thordarson and his boss were in a helicopter observing steam rising from Ruapehu Volcano in New Zealand. They were about to head home when Thordarson noticed a spume of ash. In seconds the summit crater produced a black eruption column about two and a half miles high and six miles wide, full of lightning strokes and "ballistic blocks." These chunks of flying rock, several meters in diameter, crashed to Earth in long, curving paths, leaving craters to scar the snow.

Vulcanologist Kathy Cashman spent two Christmases in Antarctica observing the active volcano Mount Erebus. Several New Zealand scientists managed to get a leg of lamb for their traditional Christmas dinner. But how to cook the meal in a snow-covered field camp? Cashman says they wrapped the meat in foil, then buried it in a canvas bag in an area heated from below by the volcano. The meat cooked well but tasted a bit like sulfur.

For eleven hundred years Iceland's many volcanoes have taken turns erupting. A tenth of the country's land area is under glaciers, some of which cover volcanoes. In 1986 Thor Thordarson was walking across a glacier, admiring spectacularly sunlit, shining blue crevasse walls, when he heard the sound of running water. He was standing on a thin layer of ice, melted from below by volcanic activity. This was a classic *jökulhlaup* (yo–KUL–hloip), a volcano-induced flood. He escaped just before water normally stored in the volcano's summit caldera (crater) rushed downward, a flash flood.

In 1918 when the subglacial Icelandic volcano Katla erupted, a nine-mile-wide flood, with hill-size chunks of ice and snow carried by the water, spilled across the plain and into the sea.

Historical records dating from A.D. 1500 seem to show that within a five-hundred-mile radius, eruptions are about eight times as likely on the day of a big earthquake. If a volcano is building toward eruption, an earthquake might trigger it.

Strange safety measures: When Ecuador's Tungurahua Volcano erupted in 1918, locals fled wearing wooden bowls on their heads to protect against falling rocks.

In 1994 volcanoes on opposite sides of a Guinean island erupted for four months, then subsided. Evacuees moved back—but then the island group began sinking four to six feet a year. Many buildings are now underwater.

Hawaii, August 1997: Lava from Kilauea Volcano flowing toward the ocean destroyed a seven-hundred-year-old temple that had once been used for rites of human sacrifice. It had narrowly escaped destruction four times. Hawaiians had long believed that Pele, the Hawaiian volcano goddess, would spare the sacred site.

More than six thousand years ago an Oregon volcano called Mount Mazama erupted. Before the explosion the mountain stood at 12,000 feet; afterward it collapsed into an enormous 1,900-foot-deep crater—what is now famous Crater Lake, known worldwide for its intensely blue waters. In the middle of the lake is Wizard Island, the result of a later, much smaller eruption.

In 1943 Dominic Pulido, a Mexican farmer living near Paricutín, watched, astonished, as a pile of ash appeared in his cornfield. After two weeks of strange ground tremors and noises like underground thunderstorms, an eighty-foot crack appeared in the field, hissing and spewing ash and red-hot stones. Then the ground bulged upward 6 to 8 feet. Pulido said, "Smoke began to rise, with a hiss or whistle, loud and continuous, and there was a smell of sulfur. I then became greatly frightened." He had good reason to be. The new mountain was 33 feet high by the next morning, 550 feet high by the end of the week. In a year it was 1,200 feet high, and by the time it went dormant in 1952, it had a cinder cone almost 1,400 feet tall. It destroyed the town it was named after.

What's the longest word in English? *Pneumono-ultramicroscopicsilicovolcanoconiosis.* It's a lung disease caused by breathing fine volcanic (or similar) dust.

There are abnormally high concentrations of carbon dioxide in the vicinity of Mammoth Mountain, a volcano in eastern California—high enough to kill nearby forest. The U.S. Forest Service has closed a nearby campsite because campers and rangers reported near-asphyxiation experiences. Carbon dioxide is seeping out of the volcano's flanks.

From 1983 to 1989 Kilauea Crater in Hawaii produced enough lava to pave a highway around the earth—four times.

Stromboli Volcano in Italy erupts about every twenty minutes. It has been erupting for more than 2,500 years. At night sailors can see the volcano's ashes glowing. They call it the Lighthouse of the Mediterranean.

Mount Pelée

Three days before the 1902 eruption of Mount Pelée that destroyed it, the Caribbean town of Saint-Pierre was invaded by deadly poisonous, foot-long black centipedes driven from the slopes of the mountain by tremors and gases from the restless volcano. The centipedes invaded a sugar mill and homes. The hordes of crawlies bit the legs of terrified horses as mounted men beat at them with stalks of sugarcane.

Even more deadly were the volcano-displaced snakes. The fer-de-lance is called the two-step snake: After it bites, a victim can take two steps before falling dead. Dozens of humans and animals died before soldiers shot the last of the fer-de-lance snakes.

May 1902: Mount Pelée had been spouting ash and fumes for a month. The beautiful Caribbean coastal town of Saint-Pierre, Martinique, West Indies, was four miles downslope. Given false assurance by a politician who wanted an undisturbed election on May 10, people were kept from leaving. On May 8 a violent eruption's high-speed ash flow—with hot gases and volcanic dust hurtling at an estimated speed of one hundred miles an hour—obliterated the town. All but two of more than twenty-nine thousand inhabitants were killed in minutes, mostly from breathing scalding ash and poisonous gases.

Pelée's ash flow was hot enough to *vaporize* victims' clothing; it melted glass windows. Buildings were leveled, and several heavy six-inch cannons were blown off their mounts. A three-ton statue of the Virgin Mary was flung forty feet from its pedestal. Masses of roof sheeting were wrapped like cloth around posts. Building girders were looped as if they were made of rope. The politician who had kept people from escaping died, as did his wife, boiled alive.

Eighteen ships were anchored off Saint-Pierre when Mount Pelée erupted. A ship's officer said the ashy shower following the first blast was like "very thin cement that clung to people like glue. The assistant purser's face and head were so weighted down with the stuff that he seemed giddy and off balance. When he asked me to break the casing off his head I was afraid it would scalp him when I took it off."

A few months after Mount Pelée erupted, a gigantic shaft of multicolored solidified lava rose from the crater, forced straight up by pressure deep inside the mountain. This volcanic spine was 350 to 500 feet thick at its base. At night it glowed with red incandescent lines. As it rose, great blocks of lava broke off from the top and crashed into the crater, but the shaft grew as much as fifty feet a day. The Tower of Pelée was twice as tall as the Washington Monument—then collapsed about a year later.

Krakatau: The Most Powerful Volcano of Modern Times

In 1883 Krakatau Volcano erupted in Indonesia. People more than 3,000 miles away heard the roar. The nuclear bomb at Hiroshima wasn't heard beyond 50 miles away. Shock waves from the blast reverberated around the world thirteen times. The volcano spewed so much ash, it fell on ships 3,775 miles away. Two-thirds of the island was destroyed, and the 2,600-foot-high peak was reduced to a hole 800 feet deep. The eruption wiped out 163 villages and killed 36,417 people.

A giant 120-foot tsunami (tidal wave) caused by the explosion hurled ashore blocks of coral weighing as much as 600 *tons*. Sea waves occurred as far away as Cape Horn, and possibly England. After the eruption new islands of steaming pumice and ash rose from a 100-foot-deep sea. Since then small, frequent eruptions have formed an island called Child of Krakatau.

Three months after the eruption a veil of volcanic

dust surrounded Earth high in the atmosphere, causing such vivid red sunset afterglows that false fire alarms were sounded as far away as New York. The unusual sunsets lasted for three years. The dust filtered sunlight; Earth's temperature fell. In England it snowed every month of 1883. Normal temperatures finally came back in 1888.

Mount Saint Helens

Before May 18, 1980, Mount Saint Helens in Washington State was beautiful, one of the most frequently climbed peaks in the Cascades. Nearby Spirit Lake was a favorite for hiking, camping, boating, and fishing. After two months of small earthquakes and explosions, the north slope of Mount Saint Helens bulged with rising magma. At 8:32 A.M. on May 18, 1980, a Richter magnitude 5.1 earthquake jolted the volcano, and the whole north side broke loose. The explosion was heard twenty miles away.

The loosened rock, soil, and volcanic material hurtled down the mountain at more than 100 miles per hour. A second mass of rock and earth collapsed behind it, then a third. As pressure inside the volcano was reduced hot magma began to froth and explode.

The nine-hour explosion spewed 275 million tons of ash fifteen miles into the atmosphere, enough to bury a football field 150 miles deep. The 600°F pyroclastic eruption traveled at up to 670 miles per hour, starting fires that burned for months. Sixty-two people were killed, including vulcanologist Dr. David Johnston; some victims were sixteen miles from the summit.

The tree-removal zone closest to the mountain was scoured down to bedrock. Trees up to 165 feet tall were flattened. Farther away, in the blowdown zone, trees as big as seventeen feet in diameter and up to 200 feet tall were knocked over or snapped in half, aligned in loose heaps pointing away from the mountain. Still farther away trees were killed by the intense heat in the standing-dead zone.

An avalanche of mud, ash, and debris followed the first blast and swept away trees, bridges, and entire hillsides. Valleys seventeen miles away were filled with rubble hundreds of feet deep. Streams flowing into the Toutle River valley were blocked by the debris. New lakes formed. The three largest are Coldwater Lake, Castle Lake, and Jackson Lake.

When the slurry of red-hot ash and rock mixed with melting snow and ice and raged into Spirit Lake, the water temperature rose to about 100°F. Millions of salmon died. People saw them jumping onto the banks, desperate to escape the heat. A splash wave surged, leaving scour marks 600 feet above the lake. In places the searing ash heated water into 2,000-foot plumes of scalding steam. Huge craters scarred the shoreline.

National Geographic magazine sent a photographer, Reid Blackburn, to document the event. He refused to take any time off, afraid he'd miss the eruption. When it came, he was eight miles from the mountain, ready with two cameras. He made it to his car, but the explosion blew out the windows. His body was found in the driver's seat, buried to the shoulders in ash. A photography award was named for this dedicated man.

Vulcanologist David Johnston saw a bluish flame in the crater and watched the bulge form. At 8:39 A.M. he radioed, "Vancouver! Vancouver! This is it!" Searchers found no sign of him. His camp—Coldwater 2 Observation Post, about six miles from the mountain—was under four feet of rocky ash.

Harry R. Truman, eighty-four, had owned and operated the lakeside Mount Saint Helens Lodge for fifty years. Gruff and stubborn, he refused to evacuate his home and leave his sixteen cats. Officials warned him. Family and friends pleaded with him. Harry was sure he could outrun lava. He told his sister he had a secret mine shaft for shelter; he claimed he would "spit in the mountain's eye." Americans admired his spirit and sent fan mail. Authorities deputized him so he could stay legally. When rescuers finally reached the site of his lodge, they found only mud, thirty feet deep.

The eruptions affected a huge area. Ninety miles away airborne ash turned noon into dark midnight in Yakima, Washington. The acidic grit blistered car paint in Wyoming. By noon it had reached Idaho. Three days later it arrived on the East Coast. In two weeks it had circled the globe.

Mount Vesuvius

In ancient times Pompeii was a coastal resort city for wealthy Romans. They enjoyed villas, temples, grandiose baths, taverns, and theaters in the shadow of the beautiful Mount Vesuvius. The mountain towered above town, its fertile slopes producing fruit, grain, and vegetables.

On the morning of August 24, A.D. 79, a violent earthquake shook the countryside, breaking masonry and decorative stonework from the buildings. Then came an ear-bleed thunderclap as the summit of Vesuvius opened. Glowing ash formed a huge, seething cloud that rose with unbelievable speed, lit from within by slashes of lightning. It churned into the clear sky as Pompeians rushed into the streets. A false midnight engulfed the town.

A fleet of oar-powered war galleys commanded by a Roman officer and famous scholar, Pliny the Elder, moved across the bay to observe and help. He died trying, smothered by ash and gases after going ashore to the south of Pompeii. His nephew wrote two letters describing his uncle's death and the eruption. His letters are the earliest known eye-witness accounts of an eruption, and the only accounts of this one. He wrote, in part:

Ashes were already falling. . . . I looked round: a dense black cloud was coming up behind us, spreading over the earth like a flood. "Let us leave the road while we can still see," I said, "or we shall be knocked down and trampled underfoot." . . . We had scarcely sat down to rest when darkness fell, not the dark of a moonless or cloudy night, but as if the lamp had been put out in a closed room. You could hear the shrieks of women, the wailing of infants, and the shouting of men; some were calling their parents, others their children or their wives,

trying to recognize them by their voices. . . .
Many besought the aid of the gods, but still
more imagined there were no gods left, and
that the universe was plunged into eternal
darkness for evermore.

After three days ash, rock, mud, and lava covered
the area fifteen to twenty feet deep. As the mixture
cooled, trapped victims' flesh rotted away; perfect
molds were left behind. Inside the molds their
bones lay collapsed.

Pompeii and the neighboring city of Herculaneum became distant legends. New towns were
built. Vesuvius erupted periodically. During recon-
struction after a 1631 eruption workers found and
saved a few Roman coins. Finally, after almost 1,800
years, the ancient volcano-destroyed cities of Pompeii
and Herculaneum were explored. In 1860 Italian
archaeologist Giuseppe Fiorelli pumped liquid plaster
of paris into the ash-coated lava molds of Pompeii's
victims, creating heartbreakingly detailed images.
Hundreds of casts have since been taken.

One observer described the body cast of a
woman. Around her lay silver coins, two silver
vases, some keys, and a few jewels. She wore a
headdress and two silver rings. Her position was

contorted, probably by pain. Behind her a woman and a young girl lay facedown. They had plainer clothes, and the woman wore an iron ring. The girl's long-sleeved dress is visible in the cast.

Elsewhere archaeologists found a sealed bakery oven holding blackened loaves of 1,800-year-old bread. Intricate, intact mosaics survived in homes. Silver work, statues, everyday oil lamps, and heat stoves were perfectly preserved. Many homes had almost every wall painted with elaborate murals from Greek mythology. Amazingly, the colors are still vibrant after nearly 2,000 years.

Vesuvius's hot ash flow preserved messages written on walls. Notes were left by shopkeepers, students, lovers, gladiators, tourists, fans, swindlers, and businesspeople:

"Someone at whose table I do not dine, Lucius Istacidius, is a barbarian to me."

"Profit is happiness."

"Lucius painted this."

"Samius says to Cornelius: Go hang!"

WEIRD TALES OF SURVIVAL

Gary Rosenquist survived the Mount Saint Helens eruption. He snapped a few photos of the wall of ash rushing toward him, then ran for his car.

He barely made it, groping through the ash and marble-size mud balls that pelted the windshield.

A couple and their daughters, a four-year-old and her three-month-old sister, camped thirteen miles away from Mount Saint Helens. A geology graduate student, Mike had carefully chosen a camp outside the danger zone and picked a site sheltered by three ridges. When they saw the immense ash cloud coming, they ran for a nearby hunter's shack. They covered the baby with a blanket; the rest of the family breathed through moistened socks. Daylight faded; the deafening thunder rumbled, shaking the ground. They emerged into a gray, hostile world and scrambled over fallen trees and through drifted ash, trying to reach their car two and a half miles away. Exhausted, they had to stop. The trail—and the forest—had been erased. The next day a rescue helicopter spotted them.

On September 13, 1989, vulcanologist Sonia Calvari and her colleagues were observing the Southeast Crater of Mount Etna through the windows of a house where they were staying. Barely a half mile away fluid lava was jetting out of the crater. When Calvari felt the heat increase through the glass, she organized a too-late departure. A mile-high fountain of lava shot up from the crater, causing an updraft that shoved the fleeing scientists *toward* the volcano. Calvari thought they'd all die. Chunks of lava six to nine feet wide crashed nearby. After an eternal five minutes the eruption subsided. Everyone survived.

After the 1980 eruption vulcanologist Christina Heliker, working in the Mount Saint Helens crater, spotted a truck-size rock balanced upslope. An instant later it toppled, shattering into hot shrapnel as it crashed downward. She fled downslope, diving behind a huge rock for shelter—and survived.

Vulcanologist Kathy Cashman was in Antarctica with colleagues to study lava-lake gases. They rope-climbed downward three hundred feet to the main crater floor, then another three hundred to four hundred feet into the inner crater. There they set up a rope pulley system to lower a professional climber-guide, then the gas geochemist. Before he reached bottom, the lava lake erupted. Chunks of hot rock a foot in diameter hailed down, sizzling the snow where they hit. Amazingly, everyone lived.

✷　　✷　　✷　　✷　　✷　　✷

The people in the Icelandic town of Vestman-naeyjar (pronounced "VEST-mahn-na-A-yar"), on Heimaey Island, were astonished in 1973 when a rapidly expanding fissure opened up two hundred yards east of town. It began spewing lava at 2 A.M. on January 23. About forty lava fountains fanned upward behind people's homes—a spectacular fire curtain. Heavy sea storms had driven more than seventy ships into the sheltered harbor—providing an unplanned flotilla of escape vessels. People crowded aboard. Within six hours all 5,300 residents were safe on the mainland. But would their town survive?

Homes were destroyed. Even worse, the lava headed for the harbor. Heimaey's fishing industry supported many Icelanders. If lava sealed off its harbor, the town itself would die. There would be no reason to rebuild it. Crews worked ceaselessly to build lava-diversion barriers, but the bulldozers were losing the battle. Then a university professor proposed spraying cold water to solidify the leading edge of the flow, forcing it into a new course. Some laughed, but the battle for the harbor had a new weapon: fire hoses. A vast seawater-pumping plumbing system was installed. For five months five hundred workers shuttled to Heimaey to work fourteen-hour days in the hellish heat; their boots often caught fire. Eight million cubic yards of cold water gradually slowed the lava's progress, then made it veer toward the open sea. It was still close; lava was within five hundred feet of closing the harbor when the eruption ended July 3.

Residents reclaimed an island that was 20 percent larger and had a more sheltered port and a new two-volcano landscape. They used most of the two million cubic yards of volcanic debris in their streets to lengthen the airport runway. For the next ten years they used the lava energy to heat all the homes on Heimaey.

When Mount Saint Helens erupted, a couple at a campsite twenty miles north were shaken awake. With lightning flashing, they fled in their car, driving on roads they could barely see, crossing bridges covered with water and mud. When they spotted a Coast Guard helicopter, they flagged it down and were flown to safety.

Only two men who remained in Saint-Pierre, Martinique, survived Mount Pelée's destruction in 1902. One of them, Leon Compere-Leandre, a twenty-eight-year-old shoemaker, was sitting on his doorstep when the earth trembled. A skin-scorching wind rose; it suddenly got dark. Injured badly, he saw others writhing in pain, dying from the heat. He awaited his own death. When it didn't come, he left his burning home. He forced himself to walk four miles to the next town, where he found help.

The other Mount Pelée survivor was Auguste Ciparis, a convicted murderer awaiting execution in a windowless underground cell. He was badly burned, but four days later he was found. He recovered and was pardoned. He toured with Barnum and Bailey's Circus as the Prisoner of Saint-Pierre in a replica of the cell that had, weirdly, saved his life.

Harviva da Ifrile was one of the few who escaped the doomed town before Mount Pelée's eruption. Her mother had sent her to her aunt's pastry shop, near an ancient crater on the trail halfway up the mountain. Harviva noticed a hot wind and tendrils of smoke coming from the pit— which had become boiling red, with small blue flames. Three people ran up the path but fell when the flames seemed to touch them. Stunned, Harviva saw the lava cover them. Then she ran.

Glancing back from the main street of Saint-Pierre, she saw lava streaming down the hillside.

People were screaming. She saw her brother race the lava and lose. She veered toward his charred boat on the beach and managed to get it into the water, then maneuvered it though a rolling cloud of superheated ashes and toxic gas. She reached a shoreline cave where she and her friends often played pirate. But lava hissed into the sea, and the grotto filled with churning water. Harviva was later rescued, having drifted miles out to sea in her battered little boat, by a French ship, but could never recall how she had gotten there.

John Walsh, head of the international division of the World Society for the Protection of Animals, often relies on rotten Asiago cheese and a dab of sardine oil rubbed onto his hands, feet, and face to gently lure and capture animals trapped or abandoned in disasters.

On the evacuation-deserted island of Montserrat the Soufrière Hills volcano remained active. Airlines, airports, and refugee-sheltering countries usually refuse animals—even loving owners had no choice but to abandon pets. John Walsh and his WSPA staff shipped in tons of pet food. Fighting the same caustic ash afflicting the left-behind pets with eye and skin sores and lung infections, they mapped the island and tried to feed every animal every day. They arranged four abandoned-pet airlifts to Florida, rescuing about three hundred animals.

Finally only one elusive dog remained, a smart, feisty, barrel-chested West Indian mutt. It was John Walsh, wearing his trademark dog-drawing perfumes, who captured it on his last trip to the island. He took it home.

Plummeting Planes

In 1982 a western-Java eruption threw volcanic ash 25,000 feet into the air. Two jets had engine stalls caused by the cloud. Both fell thousands of feet before the pilots could restart the engines.

On December 15, 1989, KLM Flight 867, descending into Anchorage, Alaska, suddenly passed into pitch-darkness—a cloud of ash from nearby Redoubt Volcano. The pilot tried to climb, but at 29,000 feet the 747's ash-clogged engines died. The plane glided downward, falling 1,500 feet a minute. Passengers and crew smelled sulfur as the pilot tried to restart the engines. After eleven terrifying failures the engines caught, and the plane landed safely.

✶　　✶　　✶　　✶　　✶　　✶

Six planes flying into the ash cloud sent aloft by the Philippines' Mount Pinatubo in 1991 reported cases of engine failure; two lost all power. In 1982 an Indonesian volcanic eruption knocked out all engines in one jumbo jet, and three out of four on a second one.

In the one hundred incidents of jet damage from volcanic ash since 1970, amazingly no planes have crashed. Volcanic clouds look like normal clouds. They often don't show on radar. Nine volcano ash advisory centers worldwide now relay eruption alerts. Airspace over active volcanoes is now off-limits to commercial aircraft.

TALL TALES AND DANGEROUS MYTHS

The word *volcano* comes from the name of the little island of Vulcano, in the Mediterranean Sea off Sicily. Hundreds of centuries ago people there believed Vulcano was the forge chimney of Vulcan, the blacksmith of the Roman gods. They believed eruptions came from his work as he forged thunderbolts for Jupiter, king of the gods, and weapons for Mars, the war god.

⚡   ⚡   ⚡   ⚡   ⚡   ⚡

Hawaiian legend says the powerful goddess Pele makes mountains, melts rocks, destroys forests, and builds new islands. When lava from a Hawaiian fire fountain is blown into fine, glassy strands, they are called "Pele's hair."

Sicily's Mount Etna is the highest active volcano in Europe. Its name comes from the Greek *aitho,* which means "I burn." Ancient writers—Hesiod, Pindar, and Aeschylus—mention it. In Greek and Roman mythology the giants—enemies of the gods—were buried under it. Trying to escape, they caused earthquakes.

Long ago the people of Nicaragua believed that if they threw beautiful young women into a volcano, it would stop erupting.

A Maori legend about New Zealand's Taranaki, Ruapehu, and Tongariro Volcanoes says they were giants, all of them neighbors. Both Taranaki and Ruapehu fell in love with Tongariro; she couldn't decide between them. Taranaki launched himself at Ruapehu, trying to crush him, but Ruapehu heated the waters in his crater lake and scalded Taranaki. Taranaki hurled stones and broke

Ruapehu's handsome cone. Ruapehu remelted it and spit lava at Taranaki, who fled down the Wanganui River valley into the sea. He now broods on revenge.

HOW BAD WAS IT: SCALES AND MEASURES

Every year about sixty volcanoes erupt, but most of the activity is pretty weak. There is no single way of measuring volcanic eruptions, but the volcanic explosivity index, or VEI, is based on a number of factors: how explosive the eruption is, the volume of ash and debris, cloud column height, qualitative description (gentle to cataclysmic), and eruption type (Hawaiian—gentle—to ultra-Plinian—very violent).

The index ranges from 0 to 8. Typical eruptions in Hawaii are at the low end of the scale (0 to 1). Most other eruptions are in the range of 0 to 2. Only four have ever been assigned a VEI of 7: Tambora in 1815, Baitoushan circa 1050, Kikai circa 4350 B.C., and Crater Lake circa 4895 B.C. In the last ten thousand years there have been no VEI 8 eruptions.

✕　　✕　　✕　　✕　　✕　　✕

VEI	Description	Plume Height	Volume	Classification	How Often	Example
0	Non-explosive	< 100 m	1,000s m^3	Hawaiian/ Strombolian	Daily	Kilauea, *(1983 to present)*
1	Gentle	100–1,000 m	10,000s m^3	Hawaiian/ Strombolian	Daily	Stromboli *(500 B.C. to present)*
2	Explosive	1–5 km	1,000,000s m^3	Strombolian/ Vulcanian	Weekly	Galeras, *(1992)*
3	Severe	3–15 km	10,000,000s m^3	Vulcanian	Yearly	Nevado del Ruiz, *(1985)*
4	Cataclysmic	10–25 km	100,000,000s m^3	Vulcanian/ Plinian	10s of years	Galunggung, *(1982)*
5	Paroxysmal	< 25 km	1–10 km^3	Plinian	100s of years	Mt. St. Helens, *(1980)*
6	Colossal	< 25 km	10–100 km^3	Plinian/ ultra–Plinian	100s of years	Krakatau, *(1883)*
7	Supercolossal	> 25 km	100–1,000 km^3	Ultra– Plinian	1,000s of years	Tambora, *(1815)*
8	Megacolossal	> 25 km	>1,000 km^3	Ultra– Plinian	10,000s of years	Yellowstone Caldera, *(2 million years ago)*

39

A volcanic eruption begins when magma is squeezed upward by deep-Earth pressure. If there's enough pressure, magma (mixed with ash, gases, and steam) pours through a weak spot in Earth's crust. Once above ground, magma is called lava.

Earth's crust is thin for the planet's size and has seams, places where the huge slabs of the surface, called tectonic plates, come together like puzzle pieces. Under these tectonic plates is Earth's mantle—dense, white-hot rocks. Twenty-five miles down, the mantle is 1,600°F. The intense pressure keeps the rocks soft but not liquid.

The tectonic plates collide, grind past each other, and slide apart. Over 200 million years, whenever two undersea tectonic plates have separated, magma has risen, liquefying as pressure decreased, flowing to solidify into new ocean floor.

When underwater volcanoes finally show above the ocean surface, we call them islands. Iceland (which should probably be called "Fireland"!) is made of volcanic rocks typical of the deep ocean floor; it has many active volcanoes.

When tectonic plates collide, one edge slides downward beneath the other, shoved down into the furnace of the mantle. Its rock softens and remelts, forming more magma, which will feed more volcanoes. This is called a subduction zone. In Guatemala a long chain of volcanoes sits atop a subduction zone. Mount Saint Helens is a subduction-zone volcano. These zones fuel the most spectacular and destructive eruptions.

Volcanoes also form over "hot spots" in the middle of tectonic plates. Hugely productive magma centers in the mantle can punch a hole in the plate. As it drifts slowly across a hot spot a string of holes can be burned through, the escaping lava forming a chain of islands. The Hawaiian Islands were formed this way; their tectonic plate drifts about four inches a year. Another hot spot, in the Indian Ocean, is covered by a tectonic plate that has moved 2,500 miles—in thirty million years.

As magma leaves the immense pressure of the mantle layer, gases that have been trapped in it escape violently, blasting hot rock into billions of pieces, called pyroclastics (fire fragments), of all sizes. Some are fine ash that circle the globe as part of the atmosphere. Others, the kind vulcanologists call bombs, can be fist-size or house-size.

Whether the magma from a volcano will explode violently or flow gently depends on how thick it is. If it is a thin fluid, the gases escape easily. If it's thick and pasty, the gases can build up tremendous pressure before escaping; that means a violent, dangerous, and destructive eruption.

The United States ranks third, behind Indonesia and Japan, in historically active volcanoes. Of the 1,500 eruptions in the past ten thousand years, 150 were in what is now the U.S. Most of these were in the Aleutian Islands, the Alaska Peninsula, the Hawaiian Islands, and the Pacific Northwest's Cascade Range.

THE VOLCANO HALL OF FAME

The Top Ten Deadliest Volcanic Eruptions

Deaths	Volcano	Year	Major Cause(s) of Death
92,000	Tambora *(Indonesia)*	1815	Starvation
36,417	Krakatau *(Indonesia)*	1883	Tsunami
29,025	Mt. Pelée *(Martinique)*	1902	Ash flows
25,000	Nevado del Ruiz *(Colombia)*	1985	Mudflows
14,300	Unzen *(Japan)*	1792	Volcano collapse, tsunami
9,350	Laki *(Iceland)*	1783	Starvation
5,110	Kelut *(Indonesia)*	1919	Mudflows
4,011	Galunggung *(Indonesia)*	1822	Mudflows
3,500	Mt. Vesuvius *(Italy)*	1631	Mudflows, lava flows
3,360	Mt. Vesuvius *(Italy)*	79	Ash flows, ashfall

More Deadly Volcanoes

Deaths	Volcano	Year	Major Cause(s) of Death
2,957	Mt. Papandayan (Indonesia)	1772	Ash flows
2,942	Lamington (Papua New Guinea)	1951	Ash flows
2,000	El Chichón (Mexico)	1982	Ash flows
1,680	Soufrière, (St. Vincent)	1902	Ash flows
1,475	Oshima (Japan)	1741	Tsunami
1,377	Asama (Japan)	1783	Ash flows, mudflows
1,335	Taal (Philippines)	1911	Ash flows
1,200	Mayon (Philippines)	1814	Mudflows
1,184	Agung (Indonesia)	1963	Ash flows
1,000	Cotopaxi (Ecuador)	1877	Mudflows
800	Mt. Pinatubo (Philippines)	1991	Roof collapses, disease
700	Komagatake (Japan)	1640	Tsunami
700	Nevado del Ruiz (Colombia)	1845	Mudflows
500	Hibokhibok (Philippines)	1951	Ash flows

Volcanic eruptions can hurl hot rocks for twenty miles or farther. Floods, airborne ash, or noxious fumes can spread one hundred miles or more. If you live near a known volcano, active or dormant, be ready to evacuate at a moment's notice.

Before

- Learn about your community warning systems.
- Be prepared for disasters spawned by volcanoes:
  Earthquakes
  Flash floods
  Landslides and mudflows
  Thunderstorms
  Tsunamis
- Make evacuation plans. You want to get to high ground away from the eruption. Plan an escape route and have a backup route in mind.
- Develop an emergency communication plan. In case family members are separated from one another during a volcanic eruption (a real possibility during the day, when adults are at work or at home and children are at school), have a plan for getting back together.

• Ask an out-of-state relative or friend to serve as the family contact. After a disaster it's often easier to call long distance. Make sure everyone knows the name, address, and phone number of the contact person.

• Have disaster supplies on hand:

> *Flashlight and extra batteries*
> *Portable, battery-operated radio and extra*
>   *batteries*
> *First-aid kit and manual*
> *Emergency food and water*
> *Nonelectric can opener*
> *Essential medicines*
> *Cash and credit cards*
> *Sturdy shoes*

• Get a pair of goggles and a throwaway breathing mask for each member of the household.

• Contact your local emergency management office or American Red Cross chapter for more information on volcanoes.

During

• Follow authorities' instructions and leave the area. Although it may seem safe to stay at home and wait out an eruption, doing so can be very dangerous. If there is time, put all machinery

inside a garage or barn. Bring animals and live-
stock into closed shelters.

• Avoid areas downwind of the volcano; remember, the gases are toxic, even deadly.

• If caught indoors, close all windows, doors, and
fireplace dampers.

• If caught outdoors, seek shelter indoors if possible.

• During a rockfall seek shelter and protect your
head.

• Avoid low-lying areas, where poisonous gases
can collect and flash floods can be most dangerous. If caught near a stream, beware of mudflows.

• Protect yourself:

  Wear long-sleeved shirts and pants.

  Use goggles to protect your eyes.

  *Use a dust mask or hold a damp cloth over your
  face to help breathing.*

• Stay out of the area. A lateral blast from a volcano can travel many miles from the mountain.
Trying to watch an erupting volcano is a deadly
idea.

• Beware of mudflows—powerful, deadly swift
"rivers" of mud. They form when rain falls
through ash-carrying clouds or when rivers are

clogged during an eruption. They are most dangerous close to established stream channels. When you approach a bridge, look upstream. If a mudflow is approaching or moving beneath the bridge, don't cross—it might destroy the bridge.

After

• Listen to a battery-powered radio or television for the latest emergency information.

• Stay away from volcanic ashfall. If you have a respiratory ailment, avoid contact with any amount of ash.

• When outside, cover your mouth and nose. A number of victims of the Mount Saint Helens volcano died from inhaling ash. You should also wear goggles to protect your eyes and cover your skin to avoid irritation or burns.

• Stay indoors until local health officials advise it is safe to go outside.

• Avoid driving in heavy ashfall. Driving will stir up more ash that can clog engines and stall vehicles.

• Clear roofs of ashfall. It's heavy and can cause buildings to collapse.

• Remember to help neighbors who need it— the elderly, the disabled, and people with infants.

Vulcanologists usually have advanced degrees in geology. Working around erupting volcanoes is hot, smelly, and dangerous, but it's also exciting, and vulcanologists often get to work in beautiful and exotic places. Their work is unpredictable; it depends on the volcano. According to one vulcanologist, "You have to be flexible to take advantage of whatever is going on at the moment. If there is an *aa* flow, then you are studying *aa* flows; if there is a large skylight into an active lava tube, then you are studying lava tubes."

Vulcanologists study a volcano's history to predict its future. Signs of impending eruption are monitored. Rumbling sounds and other clues are noticeable to anyone; other signs are more subtle. Bulges signal pressure buildup. Using extensometers to measure crater diameter can reveal early changes. Vulcanologists are now experimenting with satellite-based radar. An orbital system could monitor shape changes in every volcano on Earth, saving lives and money.

Scientists know that when rocks are heated above 1,110°F, they lose their magnetism. So if magnetic strength decreases, it means heat is increasing and the volcano might erupt soon. Vulcanologists collect gas samples from fumaroles (volcanic gas vents) because water vapor, carbon dioxide, and sulfur dioxide often increase before an eruption.

FRIGHTFULLY FUNNY AND SERIOUSLY STRANGE

Vulcanologist Thomas L. Wright, scientist-in-charge of the Hawaiian Volcano Observatory, realized many of the technical staff had never seen active lava, so he took them along, one at a time, to monitor lava advancing on populated areas. With one assistant he had to wait several times while the man found a safe place to sit and take off his boots—they had steel pin reinforcements that conducted lava heat all too well.

After Mount Saint Helens's eruption locals mailed volcanic ash to friends and family. Envelopes broke when they were postmarked and sorted, and the sharp ash wrecked postal machinery!

chapter two

LANDSLIDES

imagine this . . .

You are lying on your bed, listening to the sound of rain on the roof and the rustling of the storm wind in the eucalyptus trees. It has been raining cats and dogs off and on for almost three whole weeks. You will have to go back to school tomorrow; it makes you furious that almost all of your spring break from school has been ruined by the weird rains. The news keeps saying it's from an ocean current called El Niño. All you know is that it's wrecking your vacation.

Sighing, you roll over and face the window, frowning out at the gray sky. You love this view. The sparkle in the distance is the Pacific Ocean. Your family has lived in this Los Angeles area canyon as long as you can remember. It's perfect. Your parents can both commute to work, but here, in the steep-sided canyon, it's easy to imagine that the city is a hundred miles away—not two or three.

You stand up, thinking about calling a friend. But about the only thing you could do on a day like today is mall-walk, and you are sick of being indoors. Usually this time of year you ride your bike to the beach or swim in your family's pool. It's so gray and gloomy outside that that kind of fun isn't going to happen. You sit on the edge of your bed again and stare out the window into the backyard. In a normal year, looking up the hillside from this window, you would be able to see flowers and birds and blue sky.

Pressing your forehead against the glass, you close your eyes, but an odd sound makes you open them again. For a second you blink, confused, then you see trees far up the slope swaying weirdly, as though the winds up there have suddenly gone mad. Downstairs you hear your father shouting, and the desperate sound in his voice makes you whirl to pound down the stairs. Halfway down you make out what he is saying. He is screaming the same words over and over at your mother and sisters as they dash out the door. "Run! Get to the top of the hill!" The weird rumble that startled you upstairs is getting louder as you leap from the porch, following your sisters and mother across the street. You hear the door slam, and then your father is sprinting along behind you, still shouting for everyone to run faster. . . .

FREAKY (BUT TRUE!) FACTS

Landslides are deadly. They are often set off by earthquakes, volcanic eruptions, floods, and other disasters. All too often, people survive the terror of one disaster, then have to face another. Landslides in the United States are estimated to cause twenty-five deaths and about $1.5 billion of damage a year.

The earliest record of a landslide was in 1767 B.C.; earthquake-triggered slides in China dammed the Yi and Luo Rivers.

In 1998 a massive avalanche of mud and water erased every trace of the village of Santa Teresa, Peru. Fifteen people died, and 150 were reported missing. Those who survived faced a second nightmare: Poisonous snakes and spiders fleeing the flooded lowland jungle crowded onto hilltops along with the town's residents.

On April 29, 1903, at 4:10 A.M., 8,000-foot-high Turtle Mountain collapsed. Tons of rock crashed into the little mining town of Frank, Alberta, Canada, killing seventy-five people. The slide swept over the sleeping town and across the valley with enough force to start uphill on the far side. The mass of rock 500 feet deep, 1,400 feet long, and 3,280 feet wide closed the entrance to a local coal mine. Trapped inside, seventeen men struggled to survive. Two died, but fifteen others somehow dug through 30 feet of debris, emerging exhausted fourteen hours later. In their own language Native peoples in Alberta call Turtle Mountain "the mountain that moves."

On August 17, 1959, an earthquake in Yellowstone National Park jolted Hebgen Lake, a reservoir six miles north of the town by the same name; twenty-foot waves washed over Hebgen Dam. A million tons of water, mud, and rock thundered down Madison Canyon as the quake fractured its rock-walled sides. Moving at 174 miles per hour, the rubble—enough to fill the Rose Bowl stadium ten times—crossed the river that ran along the valley floor, then piled up, grinding to a halt, blocking surging water forced downhill by the earthquake's shock. The pooled water formed Earthquake Lake. The whole process took about *thirty* seconds.

Landslides can create ferocious winds called air blasts. Campers in Yellowstone's Madison River canyon were awakened by the earthquake. In the moonlight some saw the top of the mountain tumbling toward them. The rocky debris shoved a 100-mile-per-hour wind ahead of it that tossed terrified campers through the air.

✯　　✯　　✯　　✯　　✯　　✯

In September of 1997 a man sitting at a bar in Port Angeles, Washington, was crushed when a mysterious mudslide destroyed the building. There had been no appreciable rain for months.

When Mount Saint Helens erupted, part of the mountain collapsed. The slide moved a highway bridge hundreds of feet. The debris fills the upper fourteen miles of the North Fork of the Toutle River valley. In places it's 600 feet deep, burying streambeds and damming the water into new, soft-shored lakes. It's unstable. Every rain erodes it; some channels are more than 100 feet deep and 500 feet wide.

On July 10, 1996, a slide in Yosemite National Park crashed downward to the valley floor. Nearly 162,000 tons of granite plunged a third of a mile at over 160 miles per hour. The air was shoved outward at hurricane speeds. The wind killed one hiker and injured eleven others, and toppled many 250-year-old trees.

The 1996 rockfall in Yosemite transformed a campground into a moonscape. An inch of rock dust clung to picnic tables, cars, and tents. The pines looked like bizarre Christmas cards, covered in gray brown dust instead of snow.

In Yosemite National Park on June 13, 1999, huge boulders broke loose and fell, killing one climber suspended by his rope and barely missing a crowded campground. There was no triggering event: no earthquake, no volcanic eruption. The rocks, fatigued by weather and by hundreds of thousands of years in a precarious position, just happened, at that moment, to come loose.

In 1968 American hikers climbing Huascarán in Peru noticed a huge block of precarious ice on a glacier. They warned the government. People worried for a while, then forgot about it. When one of history's strongest earthquakes shook Huascarán in 1970, the ice broke free. It started down the mountain, skidding, dredging up thousands of tons of rock and dirt. The grinding friction of the slide melted the ice, forming a muddy mass that dropped almost twelve thousand feet through the air, then crashed back onto the mountainside and roared down the valley a half mile wide, moving boulders as big as houses. It traveled nine miles in under four minutes, averaging about 135 miles per hour, and killed 1,800 people in Ranrahirca. Part of the slide surged over a ridge, thundering down upon the ski-resort town of Yungay, killing 17,000 people.

In Italy on October 9, 1963, a landslide tumbled into the lake above Vaiont Dam, carrying more than 262 cubic yards of rock and dirt. It shoved a huge wave up the opposite bank that destroyed the village of Casso, 800 feet above lake level, then rushed over the dam, creating a wall of water 328 feet high that flooded the valley below, killing almost three thousand people. It erased villages, farms, roads, and railway tracks. Strangely, the dam itself was left intact. Had it broken, many more people would have died.

On January 5, 1999, torrential Indonesian rains unleashed widespread flash flooding and landslides. Instead of finding treasure in the tunnels they'd dug, as many as a hundred miners were buried alive in western Java in Bogor District.

Peruvians have always had to deal with terrible landslides. They have words for different kinds: *huaico* is a mudslide containing large and small rocks; a *llapana* is a smooth mudflow.

✗ ✗ ✗ ✗ ✗ ✗

In spring 1925 a landslide near Kelly, Wyoming, began when rock strata, lying at a twenty-degree tilt on the mountainside, broke free, falling in layers, making a debris dam 225 feet high. A five-mile-long lake formed behind it. A year and a half later the slide-formed dam broke; loose dirt had eroded from water flowing over it. The flood killed six people in the town of Kelly.

In Peru on Sunday, November 7, 1999, an avalanche of mud and rock engulfed parts of the Andean community of Tacabamba, five hundred miles north of the capital city of Lima. Heavy rains had apparently seeped down into soil over thermal hot springs. When cool rainwater hit superheated mineral water, an explosion rocked the ground. The boom was loud enough to deafen people for days afterward.

In 1992 a Philippine family refused to evacuate in spite of warnings that a volcano would soon erupt and could trigger landslides. They prepared themselves. By the time a lahar flow buried the lower story of their house, they had moved their appliances and other belongings upstairs. As the mud and lava cooled, they planted sweet potatoes on the newly raised soil.

✗　　✗　　✗　　✗　　✗　　✗

Lahar flows that followed volcanic eruptions in the Philippines in 1991 and 1992 clogged at least eight major river systems.

The 1877 eruption of Cotopaxi Volcano in Peru was mild, but the lahar that followed wiped out villages as far as 150 miles away.

In 1826 settlers in New Hampshire built their home and farm buildings below a steep mountain slope. When a hurricane pounded the mountain with violent rains, a landslide roared downhill. Everyone in the family panicked and ran—and all were killed. Weirdly, the flow split in two just above their house. If they had stayed inside, they'd have lived. The house and a barn—with two frightened but unhurt oxen trapped inside—were undamaged.

In February 1995 a man walking his dog at Michigan's Sleeping Bear Dunes National Lakeshore was astonished to find that a familiar 1,600-foot stretch of beautiful beach was now a steep 100-foot drop into Lake Michigan. Luckily, no one had been there when the thirty-six million cubic feet of soil and sand fell into the lake.

❈   ❈   ❈   ❈   ❈   ❈

Scientists have found more than fifteen ancient giant landslides in the Hawaiian Islands. Most happened within the past four million years; the most recent probably a hundred thousand years ago. Each slide caused huge land loss and generated waves that rolled over the land up to 1,000 feet above sea level. There is evidence that big tracts of soil and rock are loosening now. The next slide is probably a long way off . . . but the land-loss process is still going on.

In the Italian Alps is the Ticino Valley landslide area. Major slippages in 1960 and 1992 brought slides close to Lamosano. To protect themselves, residents built a concrete flume that would carry a landslide harmlessly through the village. They even provided a pump to inject water into the base of a landslide to keep the mud from thickening and piling up over their homes.

The most expensive landslide in U.S. history was in the spring of 1983 in Thistle, Utah. It ranged in width from 1,000 feet to about a mile. The slide dammed the Spanish Fork River, flooded the town, destroyed a railway and highway, and resulted in the loss of 130 jobs. Total cost? More than $500 million.

On July 28, 1999, about eighty landslides were triggered by an afternoon rainstorm along Interstate 70 in central Colorado. Summer traffic was trapped, and crews worked frantically to clean off the debris and mud.

Nearly five hundred years ago a mudslide destroyed a whaling village of the Makah Indians. For centuries it was buried; tidal erosion in 1970 uncovered it. More than 55,000 artifacts were found. Cedar canoes, ancient fishing gear, basketry, and more are displayed in the Makah Cultural and Research Center.

In January 1982 a Pacific front stalled over the San Francisco Bay area, dumping as much as twenty-four inches of rain—a steady downpour punctuated by intense cloudbursts. Scattered landslides caused thirty-three deaths and nearly $300 million in property damage. When the weather cleared, aerial photographs showed eighteen thousand debris flows in ten counties around San Francisco Bay.

✳   ✳   ✳   ✳   ✳   ✳

In 1982 mud with the consistency of wet concrete poured down a hillside subdivision in Pacifica, California, smashing two houses and trapping three small children inside one of them. The town of 37,000 was rocked by the disaster.

Landslide-prone areas are often scenic, and people don't want to leave. When northern-California officials ordered two dozen houses removed from a dangerously unstable area where ten people had died in a slide, home owners sued to reoccupy their dwellings; one turned away inspectors at gunpoint.

On Sunday, January 19, 1997, in the Puget Sound area of Washington State, almost twenty-six inches of rain had fallen. On Bainbridge Island, in Rolling Bay, about twenty bay-view homes were squeezed onto a sliver of beach beneath a high cliff. One house, where a couple was living in the basement with their children while they remodeled, was crushed by a mudslide, killing them instantly. The slide took about three seconds, scooping a narrow track only about three feet deep down the cliff face as 2,000 tons of rocks, trees, and soil fell. Neighbors heard a whooshing sound and saw a forty-foot fir tree, its saucer-shaped root system intact, standing atop the wreckage as though it had been planted there.

Slides aren't always fast, or deadly. One slow-moving landslide near San Anselmo, in Marin County, California, has lowered the road slowly—years of road repairs have been needed. Devils Slide, near Pacifica, is another slow slide. It lurches downslope and tears Highway 1 apart, then does little damage for years.

The Aldercrest neighborhood on the edge of Kelso, Washington, is the victim of a gradual, creeping fifty-acre landslide that has been destroying it like a slow-motion tornado since February 1998. Houses, sidewalks, and streets began to buckle and crumple when El Niño winter rains came, reactivating an ancient slide. One man watched his nearly intact house surf downhill 175 feet, riding a block of moving ground into the trees below. One house keeled backward; another was shredded, its roof ending up 50 feet from its framing. A sixty-one-year-old grandmother steadied herself against her neighbor's downspout and stared at one wing of the house, dangling over a brand-new 40-foot drop-off.

�‑✶   ✶   ✶   ✶   ✶   ✶

Excess water makes land unstable. A California man left for vacation and forgot to turn off his lawn sprinkler. When he returned, his house had slid down the mountain; the slide blocked a main highway.

In February 1998 mudslides caused by El Niño closed the Pacific Highway, which links the star colony of Malibu, California, to Los Angeles. Actress Fran Drescher (*The Nanny*) was rescued from a mud-closed road by highway patrolmen in a four-wheel-drive vehicle. They delivered her to a studio limousine.

Late in the evening of November 11, 1996, a triple-trailer diesel truck on Interstate 5 in central Oregon was in the wrong place at the wrong time. A torrential rainstorm had turned the land into sliding mud; more than fifty feet of the highway disappeared in a flash. An instant afterward the truck roared into the gap, crashing downward. Moments later a *second* big rig dropped onto the first one. Miraculously, no one was killed.

Every year thousands of hikers explore Sacred Falls State Park on the island of Maui, Hawaii. After a winding, rocky 2.2-mile hike through banana fields and lush forests, they find a canyon with a tropical waterfall plunging 87 feet into a deep pool. Visitors swim or picnic near the water. On Mother's Day, 1999, more than sixty people were in the narrow, steep-walled canyon when a football-field-size slide of rocks and tons of soil above the falls plunged 150 feet through the air and thundered another 330 feet down the canyon at seventy to one hundred miles per hour.

People heard a sound like thunder, then a roar, then the rocks were upon them. In the narrow chute boulders as big as cars bounced between the valley walls. One man sheltered his wife with his body and died saving her life. When the sudden, eerie postslide silence had settled in the canyon, people began to emerge. Some had missing arms, broken legs, lacerations, wounds from flying sticks. A nurse and her husband, hiking upward to help, found the scene unreal. "You'd go by rocks with blood on them, see discarded shoes covered with blood," she explained later. "But the birds were singing." Firefighters, paramedics, and civilian volunteers risked their lives rescuing people beneath the new landslide-sheared cliff.

✳   ✳   ✳   ✳   ✳   ✳

A July 12, 1993, earthquake in Hokkaido, Japan, caused a terrible tsunami and hundreds of landslides. One completely buried a two-story hotel in Okushiri.

The town of Armero, Colombia, was overrun by destructive volcanic mudflows in 1595, just after the arrival of the Spanish colonists. It happened again in 1845; hundreds were killed each time. Over the next 140 years people rebuilt the town in the same place. Then, in 1985, Armero—and twenty-three thousand residents—were buried after a volcanic eruption caused a massive slide.

On July 29, 1999, landslides toppled a key power-transmission tower, blacking out nearly four-fifths of Taiwan. People in steamy Taipei awoke when their air conditioners went off. Air sirens, set off by the power stoppage, terrified people. Radio stations worked all night to inform and calm the public.

On April 1, 1999, nine people were killed and two homes destroyed in southern Tajikistan when a rain- and earthquake-triggered slide struck Sarban, forty miles south of the capital. A recent find of thirty ancient gold coins had prompted treasure hunters to dig hundreds of holes and tunnels in unstable soil.

Five days after Christmas, at 4 A.M., a woman and her sixteen-year-old son were jolted out of a sound sleep when a landslide battered their dream home— a cabin seven miles east of Alsea, Oregon. Snapped-off treetops battered the walls as they crawled out of the house, then ran to safety. They were never allowed to return, not even to get their belongings; the cabin was too close to collapse. They saw it on the TV news in a friend's living room. Holiday decorations were strewn on the ground, and there was one shot of a *Nutcracker* figurine facedown in the mud.

Sinkholes

An odd kind of landslide sometimes happens when flat land is undermined. One evening in 1981 a woman in Winter Park, Florida, noticed that her huge sycamore tree was . . . sinking. Her whole front yard quickly followed. A crowd gathered as police roped off the area. She was evacuated. Good thing. Her *house* soon disappeared down the hole. It was followed by five Porsches, a camper parked at a car repair lot, and parts of two other houses. Phone lines were chopped free as telephone poles slid downward into the growing sinkhole. By the time it stopped expanding two days later, it was as big as a football field and was eight stories deep—and it had become a major tourist attraction. "Sinkhole 1981" T-shirts were sold. Rather than fill it in, the city landscaped it and stabilized the edges. Winter Park now has a lovely urban lake.

In February 1998 California's El Niño rains soaked and softened land beneath a San Diego freeway on-ramp. Seeing the ground collapse, Oscar Johnson jumped from his car to help a woman flee. "You could feel the ground ... trembling and sucking down," said Johnson, who stood in the rain directing traffic until police arrived. The sinkhole grew into a canyon sixty-five feet deep, twenty-five feet wide, and seven hundred feet long, filled with rushing water.

In June 1993 a one-hundred-foot-wide, twenty-five-foot-deep sinkhole opened in a hotel parking lot in Atlanta, killing two and engulfing many cars.

Fifty years of coal mining left Michigan with hundreds of miles of tunnels undermining towns and cities. In 1984 the abandoned Andrews Street Coal Mine in Jackson County partially collapsed, swallowing a detached garage, a driveway, and a car. It's easy to imagine many more sinkholes occurring in the old mining areas.

In April 1945 an abandoned coal-mine shaft in England caved in, engulfing an entire freight train and its crew.

WEIRD TALES OF SURVIVAL

As screaming villagers fled from the November 1999 landslide in Peru, some people, paralyzed with fear, stood motionless as the slide swept over them. One weeping young man who had managed to run later told a local TV station his body had felt numb, but that he had saved his mother and run, "all the time conscious that behind me, my brother was dead, buried."

The U.S. Geological Survey's Jeff Marso was in El Palmar, Guatemala, on August 14, 1989, survey-ing the Nima II River. His colleague noticed storm clouds and a column of white steam about fifteen miles upriver—near an active lava dome, Santiaguito. Fearing a lahar flow, they scrambled out of the canyon. Their driver loaded their gear and headed out, while they raced for a nearby cable suspension bridge, carrying their cameras. What began as a dull roar swelled into deafening thunder as the lahar rounded a bend upstream, and Marso wondered if the thirty-foot bridge was safe but held his ground. They managed to take amazing photos as the violent flow spit chunks of rock into the air, roaring below their feet at an incredible speed. Then they ran. The far bank was vibrating so violently that it was hard to stand up; they had to shout to hear each other. Amazingly, they lived.

Sometimes, in survival, timing is everything. In Seattle, Washington, a mudslide slammed into a freight train and threw it into Puget Sound. Two hours before, in the same spot, an Amtrak train carrying 650 passengers had passed safely.

For three long days after a 1998 mudslide that killed more than one hundred people in Sarno, Italy, a twenty-two-year-old photographer was trapped in a well, buried alive under tons of mud debris. He lay in a space roughly sixteen inches high, a yard long, and a yard wide. He felt wisps of fresh air as the unstable ground shifted around him. He shouted, praying, fighting to keep up his hope. Rescuers finally heard him. Clearly exultant, he had this to say from his hospital bed: "Living is adrenaline in its pure state. Living is the best thing. I feel like a lion."

Laguna Beach, February 1997: Waist-deep mud oozed down the canyons of this California beach town, smashing through homes and sweeping away residents. People said it felt like being in a giant washing machine, that they "swam" through the mud.

In Yungay, Peru, a man was driving past a cemetery with a woman friend when they felt an earthquake and stopped. Several homes collapsed in thirty to forty-five seconds. Just as the shaking stopped, the man heard a roaring from Huascarán, a nearby mountain. Looking up, he saw a cloud of dust and a large mass of ice and rock breaking loose from the north peak. He ran, pulling his friend along, toward the high ground of Cemetery Hill. She fell and he dragged her upright. The crest of the mud wave had a curl, like ocean surf. He estimated it was at least 250 feet high. People were running in all directions. One man just 10 feet downhill was carrying two small children. The debris flow caught him, but he threw the children toward the hilltop to safety.

One couple in the Hawaiian Mother's Day slide was delayed by a meandering puppy. If they had hiked at their normal pace instead of waiting for the poky puppy to investigate every rock, they would have been in the slide area. They heard the roar, then the screams, but the mud never reached them.

On March 2, 1998, workers were digging a canal to divert water from a swollen river. They had finished and were resting in a temporary camp when a landslide struck the area where they had been working. All were feared dead; every single man survived.

When nearly seven hundred feet of hillside collapsed on two ski lodges in New South Wales, Australia, in August 1997, a ski instructor was trapped between two slabs of concrete. Ice water from a spring slowly filled the space, nearly drowning him. After waiting without hope in the rubble for two days, he heard rescuers' voices. Their sensitive equipment had picked up his muffled sounds. Overnight temperatures dropped to 10°F. Rescuers dug for twelve hours, afraid of destabilizing the precarious hillside. The man was fed liquid nutrients by tube, and warm air was pumped near him to help raise his body temperature. Miraculously, he lived.

WHY, HOW, AND WHERE CAN IT HAPPEN?

Anywhere the land slants, soil is always on the move, slowly working its way downhill. It's a constant battle: Friction tries to keep the soil where it is, and gravity tries to pull it downward. Geologists call the process soil creep. It's usually so gradual you can't see it, but you can see its effects. Old fences often tilt downhill. Old trees tend to keep growing upright; they end up with bent trunks over the years.

Sometimes the slow creep becomes a terrifyingly fast slide. Many things can cause this sudden transformation: unusually wet weather, earthquakes, volcanic eruptions, and human disturbances like road cuts, mining, logging, or even vibration from trains. Slopes can weaken from eons of weathering, underground water, the wedging growth of tree roots, etc. Eventually, if the slope is unstable enough, gravity wins a sudden victory over friction, and a landslide starts.

There are different kinds of landslides:

A *debris avalanche* is a moving mass of rock, soil, and snow from a mountain or volcano that collapses. Volcanoes often rise several thousand feet and are made of loose rock debris. Collapse can be triggered by an eruption, an earthquake, or heavy rains, but sometimes the slope just gives way under the constant pull of gravity. The moving debris can incorporate river water, snow, trees, bridges, buildings—anything in the way. It may travel several miles or, if enough water is mixed into the debris, as far as seventy-five miles downstream.

Lahar is an Indonesian word for a fast-flowing mixture of rock debris and water on the slopes of a volcano. Lahars look like wet concrete and are full of rock debris ranging in size from tiny clay particles to boulders more than thirty feet in diameter. They usually form from an eruption's rapid melting of snow and ice, intense rainfall on loose volcanic rock deposits, or a breakout of water temporarily dammed by volcanic debris. Lahars are too fast to outrun. One full of massive boulders and broken timber can crush, abrade, or shear off whatever is in its path—people, animals, farm and forestland, roads, rivers, buildings—deadly in populated areas.

Mudflows are rivers of rock, earth, and other debris saturated with water—but are unconnected to volcanic activity. They develop in heavy rainfall or rapid snowmelt. Any sudden influx of water can change dirt to slurry, which can flow rapidly down slopes or through channels. Slurry forms with little or no warning, moves at avalanche speeds, and can travel several miles, picking up trees, cars, rocks, and whatever else it can. Mudflows often flow in channels but can cover flat floodplains. They tend to form repeatedly in the same places.

Sinkholes occur when groundwater (or other flooding) dissolves or destabilizes a vulnerable land subsurface. Limestone is a good example. Once undermined, the surface soil can collapse suddenly and violently. Some sinkholes form slowly, others are dramatic disasters that happen in seconds.

Landslides occur almost everywhere. California, West Virginia, Utah, Kentucky, Tennessee, Ohio, and Washington have the worst, most frequent landslides in the U.S.

THE LANDSLIDE HALL OF FAME

Year	Type	Location	Deaths
1556	Earthquake-triggered	Shaanxi, China	830,800
1920	Earthquake-triggered	Gansu, China	200,000
1970	Earthquake-triggered	Huascarán, Peru	25,000
1985	Eruption-triggered	Armero, Colombia	23,000
1941	Avalanche and mudflow	Huaraz, Peru	7,000
1962	Ice avalanche and mudflow	Huascarán, Peru	4,000
1963	Landslide into lake	Vaiont Dam, Italy	3,000
1512	Temporary lake burst	Biasco, Swiss Alps	600
1806	Rock slide	Goldau, Switzerland	457
1974	Rock slide and debris flow	Mayunmarca, Peru	450
1972	Mining-waste flow	West Virginia, USA	400
1584	Landslide	Yvorne, Switzerland	300

✗   ✗   ✗   ✗   ✗   ✗

Landslides and mudflows usually strike without warning. The force of rocks, soil, or other debris moving down a slope can devastate anything in its path. If you think you live in a landslide-prone area, here are some things you can do.

Before

• Have an expert evaluate your property and advise you on landslide problems and corrective measures.

• Plant ground cover on slopes; build retaining walls. In mudflow areas build channels or deflection walls to direct the flow around buildings.

• Learn to recognize the landslide warning signs:

Doors or windows stick or jam for the first time.

New cracks appear in plaster, tile, brick, or foundations.

Outside walls, walks, or stairs begin pulling away from the building.

Slowly developing, widening cracks appear on the ground or on paved areas such as streets or driveways.

Cracks open on hillside slopes.

Underground utility lines break.

Bulging ground appears at the base of a slope.

Visible changes occur, such as the formation of sags and bumps in a hillside or slope.

There is evidence of slow downhill movement of rock and soil.

Water breaks through the ground surface in new locations.

Fences, retaining walls, utility poles, or trees tilt or gradually move.

The ground might slope downward in one specific direction and might begin shifting in that direction under your feet.

If you hear a faint rumbling sound that increases in volume as the landslide nears or feel ground shifting downhill, danger is far too close for comfort and it is time to run for high ground.

• To help keep your family safe, plan at least two evacuation routes, since roads may become blocked or closed during a landslide.

• Develop an emergency communication plan. In case family members are separated from one another, have a plan for getting back together.

• Ask an out-of-state relative or friend to serve as the family contact. After a disaster it's often easier to call long distance. Make sure everyone knows the name, address, and phone number of the contact person.

During

- If inside a building, stay inside. Take cover under a desk, a table, or any piece of heavy, stable furniture.

- If outdoors, try to get out of the path of the landslide or mudflow. Run to the nearest high ground in a direction *away from* the slide's path. If rocks and other debris are approaching, run for the nearest shelter—of any kind. If escape is not possible, curl into a tight ball and protect your head.

After

- Stay away from the slide area. There may be danger of more slides.

- Check for injured and trapped persons near the slide area. Give first aid if trained.

- Remember to help neighbors who may need it—the elderly, the disabled, and people with infants.

- Listen to a battery-operated radio or television for the latest emergency information.

- Remember that flooding may occur after a mudflow or a landslide.

- Check for damaged utility lines. Report any damage to the utility company.

- Check the building foundation, chimney, and surrounding land for damage.
- Replant damaged ground as soon as possible, since erosion caused by loss of ground cover can lead to flash flooding.

TERROR TECHS, WEATHER WIZARDS, AND DISASTER DOCTORS

Some geologists try to predict where landslides and rockfalls will occur so that people can avoid building homes and businesses there. In some mountainous areas scientists can simply look for old landslide tracks and assume that new slides will eventually recur. In other areas geologists use core samples (a long cylinder of soil removed by a hollow-tube drill) to analyze soil types and try to detect subtle downhill movement. Geologists study rock layers—those that point downhill with weakly bonded layers can be slide prone.

This is a difficult field of study. Nothing happens for tens, hundreds, thousands, or even tens of thousands of years—but when it does, it's over in a flash. Scientists have to do controlled experiments to better understand how landslides work. They've mixed water with black and white sand and watched it flow down a glass-sided flume, recording the movement of the sand grains with a high-speed camera. They've mixed wallpaper paste with coal slack, and PVC beads with water, to mimic the clay-sand-gravel slurry of so many mudflows.

At the world's largest experimental landslide flume, in Oregon's Willamette National Forest, researchers have slopped together truckloads of material to mimic two of the biggest volcanic mud-slides in recent geologic history: the debris flow from Mount Saint Helens's 1980 eruption and the Osceola mudflow that reshaped Mount Rainier five thousand years ago.

Scientists spent nine years analyzing one clear-cut slope in Oregon. They tested soils, took core samples, took measurements, and set up sensors. The plan was to water the slope until it began to slide, monitoring it with instruments. They never got the chance. In November 1996 heavy rains in Oregon triggered hundreds of mudslides, including one on the much studied hillside. No one even saw it happen.

The people who study landslides have come up with ways to prevent many of them. Along steep slopes beside highways fist-size rocks can hold soil in place but allow runoff. Cement walls or rock-filled wire crates called gabions are also used.

In some areas crews drill holes in the rock and place large bolts to hold the layers of stone together. Rockfall can also be kept off the roads by terracing the slope.

Damage from mudslides can sometimes be prevented by building pits to contain sliding mud, keeping it away from populated areas. These mud ponds are built in slide-prone valleys. After a mudslide occurs and the mud dries, the dirt is removed to get ready for the next one.

FRIGHTFULLY FUNNY AND SERIOUSLY STRANGE

As the excruciatingly slow but unstoppable Aldercrest slide in Kelso, Washington, gradually destroyed a neighborhood, the home owners found strength in humor. One man, whose home collapsed, said that a neighbor used to live across the street, but now he lived downhill. Another joked, "I took everything I had and sank it into this house . . . literally *sank* it."

Many sounds come to mind in connection with landslides: roaring, crashing, thundering. But barking? The sound of bells or trumpets? If you climb certain sand dunes and stomp your feet to start the sand sliding downslope, you will hear strange, low-pitched noises that people say sound like barks, grunts, moans, booms, cannon fire, hums, foghorns, or even musical instruments, including trumpets, drums, tambourines, bells, and low-stringed instruments. Scientists at Sand Mountain, in Nevada, described the sound as a short, clear cello note. The vibrations they felt in the sand were like mild electric shocks.

Desert legends and folklore from as long ago as A.D. 1295 claim the dunes hide evil desert spirits that sometimes make sounds like all kinds of musical instruments, as well as "drums and the clash of arms." These "barking dunes," also called "acoustic dunes" and "booming dunes," have been found in the Sahara, the Middle East, South Africa, Chile, Baja California, and the Hawaiian Islands. The strange thing is that scientists can't figure out why they make noises.

chapter three

TSUNAMIS

imagine this . . .

Your father is a fisherman. On the days when he is out to sea, you sit with your mother in the shade of a thatched roof she has woven between four poles and help her weave the carefully prepared strips of palm fiber into house mats. When your father is home, you sometimes help him clean the hull of his boat, listening to him and the other fishermen tell their sea stories.

One morning, before anyone else is up, you are awakened by a bad dream. You get out of bed and slip outside, shivering in the cool air. An odd sound from the beach makes you both curious and uneasy. You run to the edge of the sandy slope and stare into the darkness. In the grayish light of predawn you cannot believe your eyes. The sea is lowering itself, the water level dropping; you can see silvery fish flopping on the wet sand. Your first impulse is to run out and pick up the fish, bringing them home for your mother to cook, but a vague memory of a sea story you have heard makes you hesitate. Instead of going forward, you whirl and run back toward your house, screaming to waken everyone.

People stumble out of their houses, and you shout the warning over and over, your throat aching from fear. You are so scared that you can think of no more to do than to tell people that the sea is emptying itself. Several of the men run to look, but your father blinks, then shakes his head fiercely, calling after them, shouting for everyone to run uphill as far as they can, all the way to the slopes of the mountain.

Taking your hand, and your mother's, your father leads the way, running, dragging you back to your feet when you fall, shouting encouragement to your mother. Struggling to the top of the steep hill just outside the village, you can hear the thunder of your own heartbeat and the gasping of your breath, until another sound mutes both.

There is a roaring from the sea below. The sky is getting lighter by the second as dawn nears. You stare at what looks like a mountain of water, moving toward the beach so fast it seems like another nightmare . . . but you know that it is not. Your father jerks you forward, and you all run uphill again. . . .

FREAKY (BUT TRUE!) FACTS

A tsunami (soo-NAH-mee) is an ocean wave—but it is so huge, so powerful, that the common term *tidal wave* creates a wildly inaccurate image in most people's minds. A tsunami has nothing to do with tides and is nothing like an ordinary wave.

Tsunamis are triggered by volcanic eruptions, landslides, earthquakes, and asteroid or comet strikes. They are vast volumes of moving seawater, a series of giant waves that can travel thousands of miles and still smash cities and drown animals, crops, and people. They often arrive trough first—that means the water level of the ocean seems to drop below normal low tide, sucked back toward the advancing mass of the wave. Then the huge, deadly, flat-topped wave comes thundering in.

Water seems soft, forgiving. But consider this simple fact: A thirty-foot tsunami exerts forty-nine *tons* of pressure per square yard.

Around midnight on January 27, 1700, Japan's wintry Pacific seas suddenly rose seven feet, washing through houses and flooding rice paddies up and down the western coast. For three hundred years no one knew why. Then, finally, a Japanese scientist put the pieces together. About ten hours before, there had been a giant earthquake five thousand miles away in the Pacific Northwest of what would one day be America. The far-flung wave indicates an epic earthquake—a Richter magnitude 9 event that must have rocked hundreds of miles of coastline. The tsunami left sand deposits in marshes as much as half a mile inland up and down the American coast. Scientists calculate that the wave was at least thirty feet high. Stories passed down for centuries by Pacific Northwest Native Americans tell of the land shaking and waters flooding on a winter's night. How weird that a Native American story and a scientific study of American coastal sand deposits would solve a three-hundred-year-old Japanese mystery.

A magnitude 8.3 earthquake struck in the Pacific Ocean in 1993, its center about one hundred miles off Japan's coast. The earthquake itself did no damage, but it set off a tsunami that raced across the ocean toward Japan, sinking about eight thousand ships. When it smashed into the coast, it flattened nearly nine thousand houses.

Disaster eyewitnesses can have trouble recalling facts. After a Peruvian tsunami some people said that they had seen three waves, others only one. For some people the waves had been silent, black, and dirty, for others the waves had looked white and had hissed.

A giant tsunami slammed into Cape Lopatka, Siberia, in 1737. The cause was an earthquake in the ocean near Japan. The tsunami left its run-up (high-water) mark on a cliff 210 feet above sea level. That's almost half the height of the Washington Monument.

On November 18, 1929, an earthquake off the coast of Grand Bank, Newfoundland, triggered a tsunami and an ocean-floor landslide. The undersea slide worsened the tsunami and had a second deadly effect: It damaged transatlantic telegraph cables. Tsunami warnings couldn't get through. Unwarned, the towns on Burin Peninsula, Newfoundland, suffered heavy damage. Twenty-nine people died—the worst Canadian quake death toll.

Survivors of a 1998 Papua New Guinea tsunami described it as being plateau-shaped waves two to three miles long and about thirty feet high. The biggest wave inundated the shore for a full minute before draining away—then the next mountain of water closed in.

✳ ✳ ✳ ✳ ✳ ✳

On November 1, 1755, in Lisbon, Portugal, a series of massive earthquakes started ravaging fires as candles in homes were overturned. Heat-dazed residents ran to the waterfront—then a tsunami, estimated at fifty feet high, swept in.

Most tsunamis are caused by undersea earthquakes, landslides, and volcanic eruptions. But every few thousand years one is caused by the giant splash of a big meteoroid crashing into Earth's oceans. Scientists estimate that a 600-foot-wide asteroid falling in the mid-Atlantic would kick up seven- to eight-foot tsunamis on both sides of the ocean. An Atlantic-strike asteroid three miles in diameter would tsunami-flood the upper two-thirds of the eastern United States all the way to the Appalachian foothills. It would drown the coasts of France and Portugal.

In 1946 a magnitude 7.8 earthquake in Alaska's Aleutian Islands caused a tsunami. At the newly built Scotch Cap Lighthouse on Unimak Island the wave height reached 115 feet. The steel-reinforced concrete structure was 40 feet above the sea and stood five stories high, and it was completely destroyed. Five people died.

✠　　✠　　✠　　✠　　✠　　✠

This same Alaskan quake sent a tsunami to Hawaii. Pololu Valley recorded the highest run-up, of more than 36 feet. In the city of Hilo it was over 24 feet high. There were 159 fatalities and $26 million in damage. Every house on the main street facing Hilo Bay was washed off its foundation and smashed against buildings on the far side of the street. All along the waterfront, houses were overturned; railroad rails and ties were ripped from their roadbeds. The coastal highway was buried, and whole beaches were simply washed away. Tsunamis can *erase* things.

On August 12, 1948, the Seismic Sea Wave Warning System (later renamed the Pacific Tsunami Warning System) was established. At last, people could be warned when a devastating wall of seawater was rushing toward them. Because it is very hard to tell which tsunamis will cause damage, warnings are sent for even the smallest. Warnings continue after what appear to be the biggest waves have passed. Many lives have been saved.

On March 9, 1957, a magnitude 8.8 earthquake south of the Andreanof Islands—part of the Aleutian Islands of Alaska—caused a Pacific-wide tsunami.

The waves traveled as far as San Diego, California; El Salvador; and Japan. The Hawaiian Islands, more than two thousand miles from the source, suffered enough damage to leave behind a $5 million repair bill. The island of Kauai was hit hard. Homes were destroyed at Wainiha and Kalihiwai. At Haena the waves were more than fifty feet high—about the height of a five-story building! Miraculously, no one was killed.

On November 4, 1952, a magnitude 8.2 earthquake off the coast of the Kamchatka Peninsula in Russia created a tsunami that caused severe damage there, then spread throughout the Pacific. On Midway Island, almost two thousand miles away, streets and buildings were inundated with three feet of water. In Hawaii the waves destroyed boats, downed phone lines, destroyed piers, scoured beaches, flooded lawns, and drowned six unlucky cows. In Honolulu Harbor a cement barge was washed off its mooring and thrown into a freighter. In Hilo Bay, where the run-up was as high as eleven and a half feet, a bridge connecting Cocoanut Island to the shore was lifted off its foundation, then dropped, smashing the heavy structure.

✵　　✵　　✵　　✵　　✵　　✵

A tsunami that hit Chile in 1868 carried ships inland almost two miles, then washed back out, stranding them there.

On February 21, 1996, a magnitude 7.5 earthquake struck about eighty miles off northern Peru. The earthquake-created tsunami centered on the city of Chimbote and affected a 360-mile-long stretch of coast. Twelve people were killed, some of them fishermen caught on the shoreline rocks. In the town of Coishco two brick walls—one of them one hundred feet long and the other five hundred—were destroyed, and houses were damaged. In Santa, north of Coishco, four people were gathering firewood and two were looking for gold on Campo Santa beach. The giant waves killed them all.

In southern New South Wales an ancient, monster tsunami is believed to have tossed ninety-ton boulders onto cliffs ninety feet high.

The 1993 magnitude 7.8 earthquake on Hokkaido affected the southwestern coast of Japan's most sparsely populated island. The quake's tsunami battered the nearby island of Okushiri, killing two hundred people. Water run-up was from thirty to one hundred feet. Modern precautions had been taken. The settled coast of Okushiri, the southernmost part of Aonae, had new, massive fifteen-foot seawalls. The tsunami washed right over them, perhaps slowed a little. It destroyed all wood-frame structures and flattened miles of power lines. Roads were undermined and stripped of concrete, the blocks of shattered cement washed far inland.

Seafloor and coastline contours influence the height of tsunami waves. During the 1993 tsunami in Okushiri, Japan, the run-up averaged fifty to sixty-five feet. Where the waves slammed into a V-shaped valley, the water cannonballed up to ninety feet above sea level.

On May 22, 1960, a magnitude 8.6 earthquake off south-central Chile triggered a Pacific-wide tsunami. On Chiloé Island, Chile, people were so afraid of the earthquake that boat owners went to sea to escape the shaking. The hissing artificial low tide that signals a tsunami began ten to fifteen minutes after the earthquake. When the plateaued crest roared in, every boat sank.

Fourteen hours later and six thousand miles

away, the tsunami rolled into Hilo, Hawaii. Sirens had warned people; most fled to high ground. Some ignored the warnings and stayed in bayside homes. The first wave, a small four-footer, came at about 9:00 P.M. The second, a nine-foot wave, came at 12:40 A.M. but did little damage. Many thought the danger was over. But less than half an hour later a twenty-foot vertical wall of water moving at 440 miles per hour crashed through the seawall and buffer zone and roared into downtown Hilo. In seconds the power plant was destroyed. The city went dark as the pounding waves tore it apart. Sixty-one people died. Parking meters were bent flat. Cars were wrapped around tree trunks. In some areas only reinforced concrete or structural steel buildings—and a few others they sheltered—remained standing. When the water receded, streets were strewn with tons of garbage, fish, mud, and the wreckage of small boats.

Along the Peru-Chile coast the estimated loss of life from the May 1960 tsunami ranged from 330 to 2,000 people, and the run-up was measured as high as eighty feet. Run-up was even noticed along the U.S. West Coast, in Crescent City, California, where it reached five feet. The first wave arrived fifteen and a half hours after the tsunami was triggered. Japan, more than 10,500 miles away from the tsunami's source off the coast of Chile, lost 150 people.

Tsunamis defy scientific analysis. One tsunami destroyed houses in a cove without damaging a house on an unprotected headland—the opposite of what a storm wave would have done.

Scientists think a huge asteroid crashed into the Gulf of Mexico sixty-five million years ago, generating a dust-and-debris cloud that dimmed sunlight and changed the world's climate—killing off the dinosaurs. It caused a tsunami probably *miles* high, cresting above the clouds! Water-carried debris from the ancient tsunami has been found one thousand miles away, in Alabama and Arkansas.

The 1908 earthquake that destroyed Messina, Italy, was caused by a shallow fault a few miles offshore. The resulting seven-foot tsunami smashed smaller boats in the harbor. It overwhelmed the quay and piers. Many people escaping quake-destroyed buildings ran dockside in the hope of leaving the chaotic city by boat. No one can even guess how many were standing on the quay when the wave washed in. British sailors heard their cries and tried to help as their ship was tossed by the immense seas. Within seconds the cries stopped, and the sailors knew it was too late. Across the Strait of Messina, on the mainland, several waves hit the unprotected shore—some as high as forty feet. One wave picked up a twenty-ton cement block and carried it sixty feet inland. Several cement bridges were moved, badly damaged by the tsunami.

THE GOOD FRIDAY QUAKE AND TSUNAMI

On Good Friday, March 27, 1964, a magnitude 9.2 earthquake in Prince William Sound in Alaska spawned a Pacific-wide tsunami that ended 122 lives and did more than $106 million in damage. The tsunami reached fifty feet and traveled a phenomenal 8,445 miles at 450 miles per hour. The biggest wave hit Alaska's Shoup Bay, in the Valdez Arm inlet.

In Whittier, Alaska, the tsunami waves destroyed two sawmills; the Union Oil Company tank farm, wharf, and buildings; the Alaska Railroad depot; numerous frame dwellings; and the railroad ramp-handling towers at the army pier. They also caused weird damage. The rushing water drove a two-by-twelve-inch plank through a truck tire. One of the waves reached 104 feet above low tide. There were only seventy people living in Whittier; thirteen were killed. In all of Alaska the 1964 tsunamis' death toll was ninety-seven, and there was $84 million in damage. Alaskan run-up measurements varied, but all were high: 79 feet at Blackstone Bay; 90 feet at Chenega; 30 feet at Valdez; and 20 feet at Kodiak.

Local tsunamis were created by landslides that had in turn been caused by the Good Friday Quake. Valdez Arm's massive slide generated a tsunami with a run-up measured at 220 feet in the inlet.

The town of Valdez, more than ninety miles from the quake's epicenter, had been built on an unstable outwash delta. The earthquake loosened a strip of land about three-quarters of a mile long and six hundred feet wide; it slid into the sea. The dock and part of the town went with it. The huge slide caused a local tsunami that slammed into the waterfront. It demolished what was left of waterfront structures, destroyed the fishing fleet, and wrecked buildings two blocks inland. Property damage was $15 million. Thirty people died—and it was all over in less than five minutes.

✗　　✗　　✗　　✗　　✗　　✗

At Seward, Alaska—a community of about 2,300, more than forty-five miles from the epicenter—the Good Friday Quake collapsed a section of the waterfront, which slid into Resurrection Bay. Waves were hurled in all directions, destroying the Alaska Railroad docks and washing out railroad and highway bridges. Railroad cars were piled up like giant steel toys. An oil spill was ignited, and flaming oil spread over the waterfront. Fires leaped to ignite railroad cars, the electric plant, and some homes. Then, about twenty minutes after the local tsunami, the first wave of the main tsunami arrived. The local and main tsunamis at Resurrection Bay caused $14.6 million in damage and killed eleven people.

Warnings came for the main tsunami, but not the local ones. Nearby cities had no warning of oncoming waves. After the Good Friday Quake the West Coast and Alaska Tsunami Warning Center was created. It can quickly warn towns of local tsunamis; it saves lives.

Two hours after Alaska's Good Friday Earthquake the state disaster office in California received warning of a possible "tidal wave," as tsunamis were then called. An hour later local law enforcement agencies were warned. Officials didn't know what to expect—the average citizen knew even less. In Crescent City, on the northern California coast, evacuations of low ground weren't begun until three and a half hours after the earthquake—when the waves were less than an hour away. First, two big waves rolled into the barely protected harbor, damaging waterfront buildings. Some residents returned to inspect the damage—too soon. Though only twelve to fifteen feet high, the third and forth waves washed more than a quarter mile inland, destroying the business district. Eleven people drowned. Massively heavy locomotives were lifted and moved several blocks. There was about $27 million in damage.

Incredibly, ten thousand San Franciscans heard the Good Friday Quake tsunami warnings as an invitation; they lined the beach to see it. Miraculously, no one was killed. The wave had lost size, and the curve of the coastline protected the foolish crowds.

After another hour and a half the first wave hit Hilo, Hawaii, where the run-up was measured at ten feet. The effects of the tsunami were felt as far south as Cuba. Harbors and waterways as far away as the Louisiana and Texas Gulf Coasts had some damage.

Education about tsunamis, and even a minute or two of lead time, can save lives. During the 1993 tsunami in Okushiri, Japan, many people were out the door and sprinting up the hill in their pajamas within minutes of the warning—and lived.

On July 9, 1958, in Alaska's Lituya Bay, 125 miles west of Juneau, Bill and Vivian Swanson anchored their trawler just inside Lituya's narrow sea channel, behind the mile-long protective La Chaussee Spit. At 10:17 P.M., during the long arctic-summer dusk, they felt a violent shudder and realized an earthquake had hit.

Staring at the bay head, where three tidewater glaciers ended and mountains rose thousands of feet out of the water, they watched a gigantic landslide. An estimated forty million cubic yards of rock avalanched downward 3,000 feet. The splash crater rebounded into a wave that roared 1,700 feet up the opposite side. It severed and uprooted trees, neatly stripping branches and bark. The force of the water removed soil down to bedrock.

A moment later the Swansons realized the wave was heading toward them at a hundred miles per hour. In the four minutes it took the wall of water to reach them, they could do little but watch in terror. When it hit, their trawler shot upward to the wave's crest, then slid backward. Clinging to the rail, Bill Swanson saw treetops eighty feet below as the wave carried the boat over the 150-yard-wide La Chaussee Spit. The tsunami flung the trawler stern-first into deep water. Hull full of air, it didn't sink. The Swansons scrambled into a skiff and were rescued two hours later.

HOW BAD WAS IT: SCALES AND MEASURES

Tsunamis are usually measured by their run-up—the maximum water-reach height above sea level. Tsunamis can usually reach a maximum run-up height of about 100 feet. A notable exception is the landslide-generated tsunami in Lituya Bay, Alaska—the one the Swansons survived—which produced a 1,722-foot wave!

WHY, HOW, AND WHERE CAN IT HAPPEN?

If you throw a good-size stone into a pond, you can see a series of concentric ripples. Tsunamis are ripplelike in shape and form, but the forces that cause them usually come from underwater and are much more powerful. Undersea landslides, the collapse of oceanic islands, volcanic eruptions, earthquakes, and impacts by comets or asteroids can generate giant tsunamis.

No one has ever seen a comet or an asteroid cause a tsunami, but computer simulations show that the giant tsunamis unleashed by Hollywood special-effects wizards have almost certainly happened in the distant past.

The most common tsunami maker is the buckling of the seafloor caused by an undersea earthquake. During a quake parts of the seafloor can snap upward as tension is released; other areas may sink. In the instant after the quake the shape of the sea surface mirrors the upheaval below. Just as quickly, gravity acts to return the sea surface to its original shape. As the sea flattens out, ripples race outward and a tsunami is born.

Open ocean waters are more than twenty thousand feet deep. Tsunami waves there approach speeds of six hundred miles per hour—as fast as a jet. They can cross the Pacific in less than a day. But gazing out the window of a 747, or even standing on the deck of a ship, you wouldn't be able to spot the tsunami among the normal wind-driven swells. In deep water the waves spread out and hunch down, usually one to three feet high, with hundreds of miles between crests. Everyday, wind-generated waves are usually thirty to sixty feet apart.

At sea, tsunami waves barely show above the surface; in open water they are gentle—even though below the ordinary-looking crest a vast mass of water that goes down thousands of feet is moving too. A tsunami's momentum is enormous. The 1960 earthquake off the coast of Chile generated a tsunami that had enough force to kill 150 people in Japan; it was still powerful and destructive after a journey of twenty-two hours and ten thousand miles. The waves from a transpacific tsunami can reverberate back and forth across the ocean for days.

Near land the seafloor slants upward. As the huge volume of moving water is forced to become shallower, it drags on the front part of the wave, slowing it. But the water behind is still shoving forward, and a gigantic pileup effect results. The water's weight and momentum concentrate in a series of towering surface waves. Many tsunamis reach thirty feet or more—some reach one hundred feet. They strike with devastating force, sometimes close together, sometimes as much as an hour apart. The lulls between waves have tricked people—costing them their lives.

Some tsunamis push a trough ahead of their crest, which can first withdraw water from the coastal shallows, emptying harbors, leaving fish flopping on the mud. If the curious stand on the beach to watch, they can be killed when the crest of the tsunami wave comes roaring in. Tsunamis can also come without any low-water warning at all. They usually don't curve over and break, like everyday waves. Survivors of tsunamis describe them as dark "walls" of water that bulldoze the coast.

All oceanic regions of the world can experience tsunamis, but about 80 percent of large, destructive tsunamis occur in the Pacific Ocean. Because of the constant grinding of Earth's tectonic plates, the Pacific is surrounded by mountain chains, deep ocean trenches, and island arcs. The seismically active system is sometimes called the Ring of Fire. The great size of the Pacific Ocean and the large earthquakes associated with the Ring of Fire combine to produce deadly tsunamis.

The deep-ocean trenches off the coasts of Alaska, the Kuril Islands, Russia, and South America are well known for their violent underwater earthquakes and as the source area for destructive Pacific-wide tsunamis.

There is an average of two destructive tsunamis per year in the Pacific Basin. Big, Pacific-wide tsunamis are more rare, occurring on average every ten to twelve years.

Ranked by number of casualties, here is the world-wide top ten (with a tie for tenth place):

Year	Run-Up *(ft)*	Cause	Deaths	Location
1883	115	Volcanic eruption	36,500	Java Sea
1498	56	Earthquake	31,000	Nankaido, Japan
1707	36	Earthquake	30,000	Tokaido/ Nankaido, Japan
1896	125	Earthquake	26,360	Sanriku, Japan
1868	59	Earthquake	25,674	Northern Chile
1792	36	Volcanic eruption/landslide	15,030	Kyushu, Japan
1771	280	Earthquake	13,486	Ryukyu Islands trench
1976	16	Earthquake	8,000	Moro Gulf, Philippines
1703	35	Earthquake	5,233	Tokaido/ Kashima, Japan
1605	Unknown	Earthquake	5,000	Nankaido, Japan
1611	82	Earthquake	5,000	Sanriku, Japan

Terrible casualties are the result of many factors. The 1896 wave in Japan engulfed whole villages and was more than seven stories tall. The Sanriku tsunami started, as many do, when the sea withdrew with a great sucking and hissing sound. It struck a totally unprepared town during a festival. Fishermen at sea didn't notice the gentle open-sea passage of the deadly wave and returned to find their families perished and the coast strewn with the wreckage of their homes.

Other Horrible Mentions

At dinnertime on July 17, 1998, villagers in Arop, Warapu, and other towns along the northern coast of Papua New Guinea felt the earth shake. About ten minutes later they heard a whooshing noise, and a wall of water spurred by an undersea magnitude 7.1 earthquake fifteen miles offshore smashed across their island. Two more massive waves followed. As they crossed the beach, the waves were thirty to forty feet high. Some people made it to higher ground, and others paddled dugout canoes into the lagoon and found shelter behind a spit of land. About three thousand people were killed, some dragged out to sea from their thatch-roofed homes and schools as the mighty waves washed over, then withdrew.

✠　　✠　　✠　　✠　　✠　　✠

In 1933 a deadly tsunami triggered by an earthquake killed three thousand people on the island of Honshu, Japan. The tsunami sank eight thousand ships and destroyed nine thousand homes.

In the United States two Alaskan tsunamis have each caused more than one hundred deaths:

Year	Run-Up (*ft*)	Cause	Deaths	Location
1946	115	Earthquake	165	Aleutian Islands
1964	230	Earthquake	123	Gulf of Alaska

LIFESAVING FACTS: HOW SHOULD YOU REACT?

There are only two things to do in the way of self-protection from tsunamis: Be alert for the alarm or another warning, and get to high ground.

All magnitude 7 earthquakes in the Pacific Basin that are undersea or near the coastline will trigger a tsunami watch. Tsunami warnings go to locations within three hours' travel of the first wave. (A watch indicates that a tsunami is possible. A warning indicates that one is highly likely or confirmed. Both alerts carry predicted arrival times for all areas in the path of the waves.) When you hear an alert, follow evacuation instructions. Before leaving home, make sure friends, family, and neighbors also know about the alert.

Warning systems will probably never be quick enough for those living near the center of the earthquake. If you are near the beach and feel the ground shake, run inland! Try to get at least one hundred feet above sea level.

Approaching tsunamis are sometimes heralded by a noticeable rise or fall of coastal waters. This is nature's tsunami warning; pay attention to it.

Big tsunamis often (but not always) make a loud roar that sounds like a train or aircraft. This is another of nature's warnings. If you hear a tsunami's roar, *run* for high ground.

Remember that tsunamis can shoot up riverbeds and streambeds that empty into the ocean. If you feel an earthquake, stay away from rivers and streams that lead to the ocean; these natural channels can condense and worsen the force of incoming water.

Where to run? Most structures in the danger zone provide no protection. The upper stories of reinforced concrete buildings (modern hotels or stores) can be safer than lower buildings or open ground if there is no time to get to high ground.

In general you should follow these safety precautions:

• Heed the warnings and stay tuned to emergency radio stations.

• Never go down to the beach to watch for tsunamis—if you can see the wave, you are too close to escape it.

• Don't go near the beach until you hear the all clear from emergency authorities. A tsunami is a *series* of waves.

• Make an emergency plan:

> *Find out if your home is in a danger area.*
>
> *Know the height of your street above sea level and the distance of your street from the coast.*
>
> *Evacuation orders might be based on these numbers.*
>
> *Pick an inland location that is elevated and know how to get there on foot or by vehicle. After an earthquake or other natural disaster roads in the vicinity may be blocked, so pick more than one route.*

TERROR TECHS, WEATHER WIZARDS, AND DISASTER DOCTORS

The science of tsunamis is fascinating and is being pursued in labs all over the world through computer simulation. Practical help for towns and cities is also important. Figuring out where and when a tsunami might strike is the job of tsunami-hazard experts. They devise ways to make sure people are warned and can get out of harm's way.

To learn more, these scientists launch computer-simulated tsunamis at digital representations of a coastline. They work to predict when the tsunami waves will hit, how high they will be, and how far inland they will reach. Officials use the maps to plan evacuation routes and guide zoning decisions.

It makes sense not to build towns and cities in tsunami-prone areas, and scientists' studies are used to plan future development. In Oregon, state law prohibits the construction of "critical facilities," such as hospitals and fire and police stations, in mapped tsunami inundation zones.

The International Tsunami Survey Team (scientists and students from more than ten countries) responds to major tsunami disasters worldwide. They try to determine the run-up height along stricken coastlines. This information helps local authorities plan locations for future schools, hospitals, fire stations, and other critical facilities. The team uses fragile, impermanent clues, like subtle watermarks, atypical or nonnative plants that might have been wave-lifted inland, as well as the memories of witnesses. To keep from burdening relief efforts, the team always carries its own water, food, and supplies.

The team is alert for any helpful data. In one area they noticed pine trees withstood the tsunami better than the local palm trees and recommended that more pine trees be planted, and that every family have a designated pine tree or ladder to climb in case they had no other choice.

Other scientists are working on ways to detect tsunamis as they are happening. In 1967 (three years after the Good Friday Quake and Tsunami) the West Coast and Alaska Tsunami Warning Center was begun.

A full-time staff of four geophysicists and two electronics technicians maintain 24/7 earthquake monitoring in a state-of-the-art facility. They monitor seismic and other equipment in remote sites all over Alaska. Their main mission is to provide tsunami warnings for Alaska, California, Oregon, Washington, and British Columbia, Canada. They also run preparedness programs, advising and training people all too likely to need it.

The Pacific Tsunami Warning Center (PTWC) is in Ewa Beach, Hawaii. Experts here detect, locate, and determine the magnitude of potentially tsunami-causing earthquakes in the Pacific Basin. If a tsunami seems likely from incoming earthquake data, a warning is issued, with an estimate of arrival times for communities close enough to the epicenter to be hit within a few hours. If a significant tsunami is detected by sea-level monitoring instrumentation, the warning is extended to the entire Pacific Basin.

Since 1948 seismographs have been used to detect earthquakes. Whenever a large, shallow undersea quake occurred, officials issued a warning. The trouble was that a whopping 75 percent were false alarms. Now seafloor sensors that can register the light touch of a passing open-sea tsunami have been added. A buoy anchored nearby relays the message to shore via satellite, and experts *know* it's time for evacuation warnings.

Some geologists study ancient tsunamis. They examine layers of sand, peat, and mud that inrushing tsunamis left behind hundreds of years before. Thick sand deposits indicate large waves that carried scoured-up seafloor sediment. The location of sand deposits helps scientists determine ancient wave size. A sand deposit on the *inland* side of a ten-foot-high ridge means the tsunami carrying it was at least ten feet high.

Is there a tsunami safety-zone listed in *your* phone book? The Hawaiian Islands are hit so often by tsunamis from every direction that maps of safety zones are printed in each island's telephone directories.

chapter four

FIRES

imagine this . . .

It's a hot, windy summer day, and you are sitting on the back porch of your family's vacation cabin. You are a little bored, but you don't mind. The smell of the woods is sharp and sweet, and the sound of the birds high in the pine trees is beautiful. As much as you miss your friends, you have to admit that you really enjoy these summer trips with your family. You and you sister even seem to get along better up here in the mountains.

The rumble of thunder startles you—the sun is shining brightly overhead. The storm must be somewhere lower on the mountain; you can't see far in that direction because the forest is so thick.

Sighing, leaning back in the porch chair, you open your book and begin to read. It's a good story and you don't look up again until you realize that your eyes are watery and irritated—like at home on a smoggy day. Smoke. You realize it, and the thought makes your stomach tighten. It is smoky, you realize—now that you are paying attention, you can smell it distinctly.

You lay down the book, wondering how concerned you should be. Your mother and father are gone—driving to the little town of Anderson's Crossing for groceries. Your sister is inside reading. You call her name and there is no answer at first, then a grumpy mumble when you call a second time.

"How long before Mom and Dad get back?" you ask, going to the cabin door and opening it to peer inside.

Your sister is rubbing her eyes. "What's that smell?"

You take in a breath, feel the raspy irritation in your throat. "Smoke."

"Is there a fire?" your sister demands. "How close?"

The fear in her voice tightens your stomach another notch. She is always reading books about disasters, and she knows a lot about this kind of stuff. Until this moment, you have always thought her fascination with calamities was a little strange. Now you are just hoping she will know what to do.

"We should walk straight down the road," she says suddenly. "Mom and Dad will be coming back to get us if there is any real danger—and that's the best way to go anyway. The open meadows down by the crossroads would be a lot safer than here in the middle of the trees if the fire comes through."

You nod. It sounds reasonable. "Where's Skipper?" you ask abruptly. Skipper is your father's dog, but you love her as much as he does. Half the time she's the only member of your family who will listen when you need to talk.

"Mom and Dad took her. She wanted to go for a ride."

"Should we take anything?" you ask, looking around uneasily; you can feel a pulse in your throat.

"I think I'll carry my diary and a blanket in my pack. And a canteen . . ." Your sister trails off, looking thoughtful. "The best thing to do is to get going fast, though."

You nod, and hurry into your room, stuffing a blanket into your pack, feeling a little silly. Blankets? Sometimes your sister is more than a little goofy. Most of your favorite things are at home—you packed old clothes and . . . You spin around, realizing that your grandmother's ring is in your jewelry box. You shove the whole box into your pack, then head for the door. Your sister is already there.

You walk fast down the road, coughing a little in the smoke. There is a hazy, strange quality to the sunlight now, and it seems like the smell of smoke is getting stronger. At the end of the driveway, the land drops away into a wide, tree-dotted meadow, making it possible to see almost all the way down to the river. Looking down the valley, you see spires of smoke billowing upward into a dark cloud smeared across the sky by the wind. You glance at your sister, then back at the fire. A yellow-orange flicker sparkles, then disappears, then leaps up again. The wind is kicking up, and as you stare the fire below spreads quickly, the smoke thickening. Without exchanging another word, you and your sister turn to run. Glancing toward the fire every few seconds, you see the sparkle of flame becoming a flickering orange wall. The wind is stronger every second, and now you remember the news shows on TV talking about the drought-dry woods this year, and how brush and woods fires are a danger.

"Run!" your sister screams, and you glance back once more. The fire is a solid front now, arcing from one treetop to the next, coming up the hill. You stumble and manage not to fall, and when you look up, you see your mother's minivan coming fast, skidding around the corners, raising a plume of dust when she hits the dirt road. Your heart leaps and you run faster, angling to the side of the road. She slams to a stop, and your father leans out the passenger side, yelling at you to stay clear while your mother gets the van turned around. You lurch backward while she spins the tires, screeching the breaks in a frantic, three-point turn that kicks up a fog of dust. Your father lunges over the back of his seat, leaning to shove open the sliding door as you run forward. You scrape your shin stumbling but manage to slam the door closed as your mother screams at you to hurry.

Breathing hard, watching the advancing fire out the back, you pray as your mother races it, the flames arcing over the road behind you, then weirdly, ahead of the car.

Bursting through a flame curtain, your mother honks the horn wildly, and you wrench around to see a confused group of deer slide past as she slows to avoid hitting them.

Five minutes later your mother turns onto the old highway, and your father whoops, leaning to kiss her, then turns to hug you and your sister awkwardly, the back of the seat in the way. For a moment you all just stare at one another, smiling. Then your mother starts south on the highway. You look out through the back window and see a helicopter appear above the ridge. "Firefighters," your father shouts over his shoulder.

You stare, wondering what kind of courage it takes to go toward a fire like that. Then the road curves and you can't see the flames anymore, only the dark scar of the smoke.

FREAKY (BUT TRUE!) FACTS

During a ten-minute firestorm a wildfire produces the same amount of energy as a nuclear bomb.

In May 1845 the worst loss of life in a single fire occurred in a theater in Guangzhou, China. It killed 1,670 people.

In California, people who accidentally start fires can be responsible for the cost of putting them out.

A San Jose fire captain accidentally started a one-hundred-acre wildfire while burning brush. He was charged $500,000. In August 1992 three hikers said they started a signal fire because they were lost—but it started a roaring wildfire that raged through an inaccessible part of the Los Padres National Forest. Firefighters battled the blaze for four days. The U.S. Forest Service announced the hikers were responsible for the $2,000,000 price tag.

Firefighters trapped by racing flames have a modern defense: shelters that are heat-reflective one-person aluminized tents. Even inside a shelter the heat can be deadly, but every bit of protection helps. Many firefighters owe their life to these tiny tents.

In July 1990 a military jet crashed. The wreck sparked a second tragedy—a fast-moving wildfire that erupted in the Santa Ynez Mountains about fifteen miles northeast of Santa Barbara, California, burning an estimated four hundred acres of forest.

In November 1998 Indian artillery firing across a disputed Himalayan border caused wildfires that destroyed more than 126,000 acres of forest. People in the smoke-infested area suffered throat, lung, and chest infections.

Scientists can look at the rings of trees to tell when fires occurred in the past. A tree grows a new ring every year—but the ring is blackened and scarred in a fire year. Using giant sequoia trees of the Sierra Nevada, scientists have created the world's longest and most detailed fire history, spanning two thousand years. Tree ring data in Yellowstone National Park shows that area has burned in the distant past as well.

One night in 1989 a hot, dry Santa Ana (an easterly or northeasterly desert wind) caused a thirty-foot pile of horse manure to spontaneously ignite in Huntington Beach, California; the smelly, spreading fire drove some Irvine residents from their homes.

Can a fire threaten national security? When wind picked up unexpectedly in May 2000, a controlled fire, intended to burn off three hundred acres of tinder-dry underbrush at New Mexico's Bandelier National Monument, became a wildfire. It raged for more than a week, forcing 25,000 people to evacuate. The Los Alamos National Laboratory, where the atomic bomb was developed, had to be evacuated. Preparing to leave, employees opened a vault to rescue hard drives containing important nuclear secrets—part of a kit to be used to dismantle a nuclear warhead in an emergency. Unbelievably, the hard drives were missing. It took three weeks for them to be found—in an area that had been searched several times. Why they were missing is still a mystery.

There are nearly a million volunteer firefighters in the U.S. These men and women respond to their neighbors' fires and save many lives every year—and prevent a lot of property damage. In some small towns a siren on Main Street is set off and can be heard for over a mile. Volunteers hurry to the firehouse wearing mechanics' uniforms, business suits, chefs' whites, and teachers' dresses—then change into firefighting gear in seconds.

On August 14, 1933, fires in western Oregon ignited the Great Tillamook Burn. Winds on August 24 fanned 1,600-foot-high flames that destroyed 200,000 acres in less than a day. After the firestorm, pastures in Tillamook County lay under three feet of ash.

Residents of New Jersey's Pine Barrens call April 20, 1963, Black Saturday. Near the Lebanon State Forest flames moved nine miles in only six hours. In eleven days the flames consumed more than 200,000 acres, killing seven people and leaving nearly a thousand homeless.

On August 7, 1997, a Los Gatos, California, man saved his town with a garden hose. During a wildfire he stood on top of his condo complex putting out scattered fires as they started from the windblown embers landing on the roof. His bravery stopped the blaze's march toward downtown homes and businesses.

Every year, usually in the fall, a hot, dry wind from the high desert sweeps westward across southern California. It accelerates through narrow canyons and has been clocked at up to one hundred miles per hour in Cajon Pass. It gets hotter as it loses altitude, warming about five degrees Fahrenheit for every thousand feet it drops. The wind is called the Santa Ana. It dries skin, cracks lips, and irritates people's nerves. Wildfires are common during a Santa Ana. The dry wind can whip a spark into a brush fire and drive flames for miles with the force of a flamethrower.

In 1961 a fire driven by hot, dry Santa Ana winds destroyed nearly five hundred homes in Bel Air, California, including those of actors Cliff Robertson, Burt Lancaster, and Zsa Zsa Gabor.

On April 21, 1982, a Santa Ana blew power lines together, causing a shower of sparks that ignited a fire that then burned an Anaheim, California, neighborhood, driving out 1,200 people.

Weirdly, trees often benefit from fires. Periodic fires reduce competition, killing nonnative plants. Some tree seeds *need* fire. The cones of many lodgepole pines will release their seeds *only* after they are exposed to fire. Thick bark helps Douglas fir and giant sequoia trees resist ground fires. Aspen and other trees do burn but will resprout from their roots. Burning kills invading weeds. Controlled fires are used to "weed" Midwestern oak forests.

Canada's October 7, 1825, Great Miramichi Fire raged for nearly three weeks, sweeping through forests and countryside with a front 70 to 140 miles wide. It burned six thousand acres and left more than 15,000 people homeless. People fled to the river, clinging to logs and rafts, but violent winds and rough water drowned many. Desperate lumberjacks rode log booms downriver beneath an arching tunnel of fire. Death estimates reached 500; 130 bodies were found.

On Saturday, September 1, 1894, the Hinckley Fire assaulted east-central Minnesota. In four hours it consumed six towns, turned 480 square miles of forest and countryside into charred wasteland, and killed 418 people. A railroad crew saved 300 lives by backing Train Number Four, the Duluth Limited, six miles through flames. The metal cars heated up; anyone touching exposed steel was burned. Others survived by crouching in a four-foot-deep quarry pond to wait out the blaze. Afterward survivors found the intense fire had *melted* railroad tracks— there were puddles of hardened steel.

New York City installed the first fire hydrant in 1908. As more were put in, America's urban fires became less murderous. Forest fire fighting has improved too but remains difficult.

✗　　✗　　✗　　✗　　✗　　✗

It was the middle of winter, during the worst ice storm of the season. Northeastern Oklahoma police officer Ron Pack was sent to check on a grass fire. He found the ground glazed over, the weird fire blazing—*beneath* the ice, evaporating it as it spread.

In November 1999 a prairie fire swept through Outlook, Montana, driving two hundred people from homes and farms. Instead of trying to save her possessions, the post office manager loaded mail in her pickup and fled just ahead of the wind-driven blaze.

The Outlook fire drove a wall of tumbling flame through town in minutes, destroying twenty-four homes, four grain elevators, parts of several farms— and every business on Main Street. Spared were two churches and the town bar, the Hub. The town's only school survived, though flames came within a few feet. Carl Tange was plowing firebreaks when wind-fueled flames rocketed past. He wasn't hurt; even his tractor was unscathed.

A pumper truck can pump 1,250 gallons of water per minute. That's 20,000 eight-ounce glasses of water every sixty seconds!

✗　　✗　　✗　　✗　　✗　　✗

In Indonesia farmland is cleared by the slash-and-burn method. Fires often spread through smoldering underground peat deposits; the smoke can be deadly. In 1997–98 smoke enveloped large parts of Southeast Asia. Outdoor work halted, airline flights were cancelled, and respiratory illnesses plagued residents.

The acres "destroyed" by a wildfire aren't really ruined. Fire recycles. Vegetation becomes ash that fertilizes plants. Within a few years after a 1994 fire Storm King Mountain, where fourteen firefighters died, turned green again. This is typical. Fire spurs a thick, green grass crop. Deer and bison thrive for a season or two as the trees reseed and recover. "Destruction" often really means "renewal" after wildfires.

Wild animals die in wildfires, but many escape. Deer, bears, zebras, lions, kangaroos—the fleetest animals can often manage to outrun wildfires. Smaller animals, like mice, shrews, snakes, lizards, and tortoises, often find shelter underground. Firefighters going in to put out lingering hot spots often report seeing unhurt animals, even after the worst fires.

✗　　✗　　✗　　✗　　✗　　✗

In April 1999 a massive forest fire raged in drought-ravaged northern China. It hadn't rained in seven long months, and the three thousand soldiers fighting the fire had no water—they had to cut trenches and beat the fire out with shovels. Finally an aircraft seeded the clouds, and on April 9 the artificially induced rain quenched the fires. Strangely, just before the fire-producing drought began, the area had suffered a major flood that killed four thousand people.

The 1988 fires in Yellowstone National Park received worldwide news coverage. Many think the fire was one of America's worst. It wasn't, by far. Yellowstone is beloved by millions of people worldwide who have visited it, so even though human and monetary losses were relatively low, the fire made the news.

In April 1999 an erratic wildfire devoured more than 130,000 acres of Florida's Everglades. Officials think it was ignited by heat from a car's catalytic converter. The blaze was named the Deceiving Fire because shifting winds helped it fool firefighters many times as they tried to contain it.

✷   ✷   ✷   ✷   ✷   ✷

In August and September 1999 the Willow Fire, started by an illegal campfire in the San Bernardino Mountains, scorched more than 63,000 acres. The cost of fighting it—with 2,700 firefighters—reached almost $6 million.

The oddest things can make a fire worse. In the ten hours that a 1991 fire roared through Oakland and Berkeley Hills, California, it ignited a building every eleven seconds. Fire departments from other towns tried to help, but the hose connections of many trucks would not fit Oakland's fire hydrants.

THE PESHTIGO FIRE

Residents of the busy logging town of Peshtigo, Wisconsin, were used to forest fires. In dry weather farmers always plowed bare-dirt firebreaks around their houses. The railroad tracks were checked for fires started by steam-engine sparks. But 1871 was the driest year anyone could remember. Sunday morning, October 8, a huge fire swept toward town.

People were terrified, afraid to run for the river, unsure if they had time—uncertain the river was deep enough. When they decided to try, one old woman refused to go; she knelt to pray beside a tree stump.

At the river some people stood like statues on the banks, afraid of the water. Many thought the end of the world had come. A priest, Father Pernin, pushed people into the water. As the fire roared closer tongues of flame arched overhead. People ducked under the water, coming up in the searing heat just long enough to breathe. Some soaked quilts to cover their heads. The cloth steamed and dried in seconds in the furnace heat of the fire, often bursting into flames. Still—hair, eyelashes, and eyebrows singed—many managed to survive in the river.

Townspeople farther from the river sought shelter on open ground. Twenty-one people from three families raced into a field with only a single quilt for protection. The women and smaller children got under the quilt. The men wet down the fabric. All the heroic men died; everyone beneath the quilt survived.

After the fire passed, people returned to the smoking remains of their town. The old woman they had left praying was alive and well. The fire had gone around her. Many were less fortunate. The Peshtigo Fire claimed almost twelve hundred lives—the second-worst loss of life from any recorded fire.

Even after the huge fire was over, smoke from thousands of smoldering flames in the forests blanketed the land. A lake steamer bringing supplies found the port by following a booming sound—men repeatedly dropping heavy planks on the dock.

THE BIG BLOWUP

On August 20, 1910, gale-force winds in northeast Washington, northern Idaho, and western Montana drove a forest fire that came to be called the Big Blowup.

In 1910 there were few trails and fewer roads. Firefighters had to travel up to sixty-five miles through rough country to get to the fires they were trying to fight.

A forest ranger described the blaze: "The fire was coming on fast, already it was beginning to throw shadows in the camp, and we could hear a rumble like a railroad train crossing a bridge. I roused the men up and ran out into the creek to see what our chances were. . . . It was light as day now in the camp." Trees crashed around them. The smoke lifted a little on the west side of the creek, and they saw a whirlwind of fire a thousand feet high.

The fire destroyed the Montana towns of Taft,

Deborgia, Haugan, and Tuscor. It killed eighty-five people and burned more than three million acres of forest—some seven to eight billion feet of timber.

On the West Fork of the Big Creek of the Saint Joe River eighteen panic-stricken firefighters, choking on smoke, crowded into a one-room cabin, huddling on the floor. But the roof collapsed, driving them back outside to try to find a way through the fire line. They couldn't. All eighteen died in the terrific heat. The rest of their sixty-man crew found safety in a burned-over area.

Backfires (fires set deliberately ahead of the edge of the blaze to create a fuel-free area) were set by men fighting to save the town of Avery, Idaho, from the Big Blowup. One said, "An impassable wall of fire was eating its way down the hillside. Our backfire . . . was creeping up toward it. In exactly four and one-half minutes . . . the two met . . . with a roar that must have been heard miles away. The tongues of fire seemed to leap up to heaven itself and after an instant's seething sank to nothingness. . . . We sank down and lay there in the ashes babbling incoherent thanks to God."

As dangerous as the Avery area was that night, things were worse elsewhere. A group of people tried to escape by train. One witness said, "Bridges behind them were crackly with fire; way ahead another burst into flames. There was no way they could make it back to the Saint Paul Tunnel or Falcon and Marshall." The train made it through the first wave of fire, varnish blistering in the intense heat, then had to turn back. A passenger, Lieutenant Lewis, wrote a report: "The flames seemed to be over a mile and a half high. We traveled back and forth. . . . Progress was constantly impeded by landslides or rocks, or burned logs." At 5:30 A.M. on Monday, August 22, the train arrived back in Avery. Incredibly, most of its passengers survived.

WEIRD TALES OF SURVIVAL

Firefighters everywhere shudder when anyone mentions the Storm King Mountain tragedy of July 1994. Fourteen firefighters, including members of the elite smoke-jumper and hotshot crews, were lost. Those who lived told the tale. They had been sent to the bottom of a steep ridge to contain an unthreatening 20-acre fire. At midafternoon a storm front moved in, and tedium turned to terror. Shifting winds whipped the fire into an inferno that covered 2,200 acres. "We saw the smoke building up, then *wham*! The mountain was on fire," said a twenty-one-year-old student who was earning college money by fighting summer wildfires. Radios crackled; someone was screaming, "Go. Run. Go!"

Flames licking at their backs, forty-seven fire-fighters struggled up the steep slope through waist-deep brush, pinion pines, juniper, and cheat grass. Leaving a ragged trail of discarded tools and equipment, they ran, knowing the whole hillside could explode into an inferno any second. Their lungs seared; they tried to help one another. One man recalled passing a comrade whose body had been blackened into a charred heap. Another described the roar as "a combination of jet engine, freight train, tornado and hurricane." Luck—and a few seconds' time—separated the living from the dead. Most who died were farther downslope. They simply could not run fast enough.

During the Yellowstone National Park fires of 1988 a group of firefighters were reassigned to protect the log buildings of Silver Tip Ranch, an exclusive, private retreat. After having eaten packaged rations in the woods, they were excited about meals prepared by the retreat's chef. Approaching the ranch on foot, they were ambushed by a huge fire-storm, driven by seventy-mile-per-hour winds, with three-hundred-foot flames and fireballs shooting up into the clouds. With fist-size embers raining down, the crew ran through blazing woods to the ranch. Frantically they fought the fire with the help of helicopters carrying water. When cyclonic winds began snapping trees, the crew chief gave up. He ordered his crew into a sparsely grassed twenty-acre clearing. The firefighters unpacked their one-man fire shelters and lay facedown on the ground, holding the heat-resistant foil pup tents over them-selves with hand and foot straps. The crew chief had no time to set up his own shelter. The firestorm raging, he lay down as the flames roared past. The meadow's sparse grass saved them all. Weirdly, the ranch survived too. The complex wind currents carried the fire to only one building and a horse-drawn wagon.

A Montana fireman on his way to a summer grass fire wore his boots and protective coveralls. Uncomfortable in the midday heat, he rolled up his sleeves before he climbed atop the truck. About three hundred yards from the fire the driver real-ized they couldn't fight it from that angle. In the seconds it took to turn around, a thirty-foot wall of fire closed in. The fireman climbed down onto the running board opposite the flames. Even there the heat was overwhelming. Instinctively he covered his face with his bare hands—and fell. He stumbled upright and ran, desperate to escape the heat and smoke. In moments, with the fire so intense he was sure he'd never make it, he remembered what he had taught schoolchildren in his fire-prevention appearances: Stop, drop, and roll. He stayed low, rolling to put out his smoldering clothing, until the fire had passed over him. His hands, face, and arms were badly burned, but he survived. Remember his rolled-up sleeves? He wrote an article for fire-fighters about proper protective clothing: "It will save you a lot of pain!"

In October 1996 eight-year-old Larry VanDen-Handel was excited about his first camping trip—three days with his dad and uncle in California's Ventana Wilderness. When they were trapped by fire, there was no place for a rescue helicopter to land. Four firefighters slid down a rope from the hovering craft, carrying chain saws. They cut a clearing so another chopper could make the rescue. Amazingly, all survived!

* * * * * *

Most of the people who survived the 1871 fire in Peshtigo, Wisconsin, ran to the river. Some drowned in the swift water or were swept against the burning dam downstream. But five-year-old Carrie Heidenworth saved herself by grabbing the horn of a cow that was swimming past her, and hanging on.

April 15, 1994: Sometimes survival takes a long time and the turning point comes in a hospital, months after the fire. Nearly six months after trying to rescue a friend from the 1993 Topanga Canyon fire in California—getting burned so badly that doctors gave him "zero percent" chance of surviving—Ron Mass left the hospital to cheers from tearful family and friends.

During the 1910 Big Blowup in Idaho and Montana a forest surveyor held his terrified crew at gunpoint to keep them from trying to flee a fire they could not possibly outrun. They made a stand at a small creek: "All our trust and hope was in the little stream and the friendly gravel bar." Some of the crew tried to hide under wet blankets, but falling snags (dead limbs) drove them out. They had buckets and doused surrounding trees as high as they could throw water. Just downstream from the desperate men an old logjam of an acre or more of piled deadwood became a roaring furnace. If the wind had changed, a blast of killing heat would have finished them. They lived.

During the same horrific fire a forest ranger guided his forty-five-man crew through darkness and a raging inferno driven by hurricane-force winds and found an old mine tunnel for shelter. The timbers at the entrance caught fire over and over as the blaze raged above ground. The ranger found water seeping into the mine tunnel and soaked blankets to hang over the opening, drenching the burning timbers. Many of his men passed out in the heat and smoke, and finally so did he. Hours later he heard someone saying he was dead. He sat up and argued the point as he breathed in the fresh air circulating through the mine. The fire was over. Five of his men had died in the tunnel, but his ordeal was just beginning. "We had to make our way over burning logs and through smoking debris. When walking failed us we crawled on our hands and knees. How we got down I hardly know . . . all of us hurt or burned. I was blind and my hands were burned from trying to keep the fire out of the tunnel. Our shoes were burned off our feet." He was honored as a great hero.

On November 1, 1999, after a fire at the Ocean City Aquarium in New Jersey was finally put out, firefighters were amazed to find a few survivors slithering out of the ash. Survivors included twenty turtles, four alligators, eight crocodiles, three boa constrictors, two pythons, and a moray eel. The aquarium's owner put the four alligators in the back of his car, took them home, and kept them in his bathtub until a better enclosure could be found.

On Sunday, August 3, 1997, the Logan Fire, a human-caused tragedy, erupted in the Los Padres National Forest in California. Dense brush, sweltering hot weather, and a dry northeasterly wind helped push a blaze across nearly fifty thousand acres. Near the city of Santa Maria one engine crew was ordered back, but fire trapped them. They used the hose to wet down brush and dirt around the fire engine. Dazed by heat and smoke, they could not get into the cab. They crawled under the bumper and set their hose nozzle to blast out a fog of water. The heat blistered the paint on the engine, but the firefighters lived.

In that same fire two helicopters worked hot spots while bulldozers made a firebreak. Wind shifts changed the direction of the fire. The dozer operators got into their heat-protected cabs but might not have survived if a helicopter hadn't airlifted them minutes before flames engulfed the ridge.

On December 20, 1977, young California reserve firefighter Joe Valencia was happy to fill in for one of the regulars—his goal was to become a regular himself. It was perfect fire weather—two years of drought. The hills were covered with paper-dry brush. A hot, dry Santa Ana wind was gusting up to eighty miles per hour. A downed power transformer near Vandenberg Air Force Base sparked a fire. With the rest of the crew, Joe donned yellow fire-retardant coveralls, coat, and helmet. He was part of a strike team: at least four engines, three brush trucks, a hotshot crew, bulldozers, and twenty-five men. The brush truck Joe was in carried 250 gallons of water and other heavy equipment—and still the ferocious winds rocked it. Joe was nearly swept away by gusts when he got out, his helmet almost torn from his head. Walls of swirling flames seemed to disintegrate the chaparral and brush. Joe scrambled back into the truck cab as the air vibrated with a strange crackling and tearing sound. Abruptly, the brush truck was engulfed in flames, superheated air, and black smoke. Terrified, Joe could only curl into a fetal position and put a wet bandanna over his face. He remembers wondering if the gas tank might explode. Time crept past, burning brush hurtling against the truck. Gradually the smoke lightened. Joe began to think his ordeal was over. But it was just getting started.

The men in the truck had all survived, but a firefighter running a bulldozer had been badly burned. Joe was ordered to accompany him in the ambulance. As it rolled away from the fire Joe sat close to reassure the burned man as the medic began to remove charred clothing. When the ambulance slowed, Joe glanced out the front window.

Flames were licking at the hood. Visibility was suddenly zero. Wind battered the ambulance, and Joe was afraid the windows wouldn't hold—or that the vehicle would be blown off the road. The heat increased. The rubber window seals burned and turned to ash, exposing the tiny space between window and frame. The wind shoved sparks through the tiny cracks. Joe turned off the victim's oxygen supply bottle, afraid of an explosion.

A sudden burst of wind and flames shifted the ambulance sideways. For a moment it became dark and quiet. Then a low rumbling sound swelled as a raging inferno leaped across the road. Joe snuffed out sparks with his gloves. The burn victim was screaming for help. Joe knew that if windows broke, the heat would kill them all. They had to move, but how? The smoke was too thick to see through.

Frantic, Joe looked out the rear window and was just able to make out the white line on the road. He shouted at the driver to try backing up. As the ambulance eased into reverse Joe shouted directions, guided by the barely visible line. Once they were finally out of the firestorm, they could see well enough to turn around and head for the hospital. Joe—a replacement for a regular firefighter—had earned his day's pay ... and then some.

On August 5, 1949, an eighteen-man smoke-jumper crew and a forest ranger were moving toward the Missouri River, working their way down Mann Gulch in Montana's Helena National Forest. A fire blazed high on the northern slope and they had expected it to burn upward, but something (probably downdrafts from the thunderstorm that started the fire) had set smaller fires in the canyon mouth, blocking their path to the river. The foreman realized he had to get his crew to the south slope, where stretches of rock and thinner vegetation would slow the fire. He ordered his crew to run for their lives.

The fire was only a hundred yards behind them, swirling through the grass, when the foreman had his fleeing crew drop their heavy gear. It wasn't enough; the fire was still gaining on them. Desperate, he took out a book of paper matches and began setting the grass on fire where he stood, shouting at his men to come close. They refused and kept running. Only two survived; they were both strong, fit teenagers who took the steepest, shortest route up the slope, found a crevice in the cliff, and climbed to the ridge and safety. These two watched their "crazy" foreman, now in the middle of his own little backfire. He wet a handkerchief with his canteen, covered his mouth and nose, then lay facedown in the hot ashes. In the tense minutes of the fire's passing, fierce winds lifted him off the ground three times. The fire didn't burn him; it couldn't come close enough over the already blackened ground.

He survived because he had "burned a hole in the fire." Today his desperate invention is called an escape fire; it has saved many lives.

In 1984 Australian firefighters fitted a protection system to a fire tanker. It was simple in concept: two spray bars aimed to spray water over the cab and the pump to keep both crew and equipment safe from heat. In 1990 firefighters reached a housing development a half mile from the assigned fire. Within minutes a spot fire was leaping erratically, and they were trapped between two fires. They knew the hot updraft soaring from the fires would bring a massive downdraft rushing inward—right where they were. That downdraft would bring fire with it.

They got into an emergency protection posture inside the cab and turned on the pump full strength just in time. Fire engulfed the tanker, the emergency beacons melted, the plastic door trim melted, the paint blistered, and the radio aerial caught fire. But the spray bars kept the cab damp. The firefighters walked away—alive and grateful.

Not all survival stories are about humans. Emergency Animal Rescue Service (EARS) is a group of more than 2,500 volunteers who rescue pets, live-stock, and even wild animals during disasters. During the California wildfires of 1986 EARS founder Terri Crisp rescued a miniature pony by coaxing it into the backseat of a Mercedes sedan.

In August 1988 Nancy Rencken was crew boss of a Washington State fire-fighting crew sent to Idaho to fight the Eagle Bar Fire in Payette National Forest. They worked along a bulldozer-cleared "cat line" and soon realized their maps were faulty. Radioing in, they could only wait while superiors figured out where they should go. Rencken was uneasy. No one seemed to know where the fire was or where it was headed. Finally she was ordered to take cover in one of the area's many meadows.

Rencken reviewed shelter use—not everyone was familiar with the heat-reflective one-person aluminized tents. She selected a safety zone an acre wide. She could see flames in several directions as she moved her crew to the open place, terrified this might turn into every firefighter's nightmare.

The crew hurried to dig places for their shel-ters—and saw the advancing wall of flame. Fire-fighters familiar with the shelters helped those who weren't, laughing and joking, keeping one another's courage up. The inferno blast hit like the roar of a tornado. Inside her own shelter, Rencken was terrified but fought to keep her head—and to hold her tent down. The fire's updrafts jerked at the shelter. Embers came in under the edges; Rencken patted them out with her hands. The shelter got nausea-inducingly hot—through the pinholes in the metallic fabric she could see the orange glow of the raging fire.

When the blast subsided, they were alive. Rencken called to her crew on the radio and had them yell to one another to make sure all were okay. The people at the outside of the group had taken the brunt; one firefighter was burned, though not too badly.

Another blast came, followed by several more. Rencken kept up radio communication. She yelled to the people nearby. The burn victim inhaled smoke and was choking. A crew member ran to help but was driven back to his shelter as the firestorm hit again.

They stayed in the shelters until numbed legs and cramping muscles and the pain of lying on rocky ground overcame the fear of what remained of the fire. The smoke was still bad. Rencken made people get back into their shelters after a short break.

Around 3 A.M. their division supervisor ordered them to a bigger safety zone. It was a long walk down the cat line in the middle of the night. The new, ten-acre safety area seemed huge to the weary firefighters. A crew already there was overjoyed—they had thought Rencken's team was dead. When the fire burned nearby again, it had slowed and calmed. The crews stood close to some of the burning trees, warming up in the predawn chill. All survived the night.

HOW BAD WAS IT: SCALES AND MEASURE

There is no formal or scientific rating for forest fires. The word *conflagration* used to mean "a raging, destructive fire"—often one burning in extremely dry, windy weather. The term is also used when a wildland fire burns into a wildland-urban interface, destroying buildings as well as trees. Fires that devastate cites are often called conflagrations. The Chelsea, Massachusetts, fire in the late 1970s was a conflagration, as was the Great Chicago Fire of the nineteenth century. If the right weather and climatic conditions exist, a conflagration can continue building in intensity and form a fire-storm.

The term *firestorm* is used when the heat, gases, and motion of a growing fire begin to create their own weather and wind. Firestorms create monster updrafts and airflow that pulls air into the base of the fire. Once it establishes this kind of airflow—called convection currents—a fire begins to feed itself, forming towering, tornado-like vortices of flame. Winds in a firestorm can top 120 miles per hour. These fire whirls can hurl flaming logs and burning debris miles away, setting more fires.

WHY, HOW, AND WHERE CAN IT HAPPEN?

There are only two causes of wildfires: nature and humans. A drought spell followed by a lightning storm is one common natural cause. Human causes are a careless match, a tossed cigarette, an untended campfire, or deliberate malice. Occasionally nature and man team up to create wildfires. In 1993 strong Santa Ana winds downed power lines in southern California, sparking an uncontrollable wildfire that burned for nine days.

Firefighters classify wildfires:

Surface fires burn grass, shrubs, and plant material

like leaves and fallen bark on the ground. These fires travel fast but are easy to control.

A *crown fire* burns in the tops (or crowns) of trees and is usually hot and destructive. Crown fires come in two types: A *dependent crown* fire happens when heat and embers from surface fires ignite the tops of adjacent trees—usually when winds are low and trees are spaced far apart. *Running crown fires* burn hot, travel fast, and change direction following wind or land slope.

Ground fires burn unnoticeably underground. They smolder through peat deposits or matted leaves and spread slowly but may pop out of the ground anywhere and cause damage.

Fire is a chemical reaction. When enough heat is applied to a fuel source in the presence of oxygen, energy is rapidly released. Heat, fuel, and oxygen are known as the fire triangle. When these are brought together in the right proportions, a fire ignites. If any of the three falls below a certain level, a fire cannot burn. To fight a fire, break the triangle. Firefighters remove fuel by setting backfires or bulldozing firebreaks. Dropping water on fire reduces the temperature. Dropping fire retardants coats the fuels so oxygen can't get to them. All these techniques slow, then eventually put out, fires.

THE FIRE HALL OF FAME

Killer United States Fires ★

Year	Location	Deaths
1871	Peshtigo, WI *(forest fire)* ★	1,182
1903	Iroquois Theater, Chicago, IL	602
1942	Cocoanut Grove, Boston, MA	491
1894	Hinckley, MN *(forest fire)*	418
1918	Cloquet, MN *(forest fire)* •	400
1900	Docks, Hoboken, NJ	326
1930	Penitentiary, Columbus, OH	320
1876	Theater, Brooklyn, NY	295
1871	Chicago, IL †	250
1940	Dance hall, Natchez, MS	198
1908	School, Collingwood, OH	176
1908	Rhoads Theater, Boyertown, PA	170
1944	Ringling Brothers Circus, Hartford, CT	168
1977	Nightclub, Southgate, KY	164
1911	Triangle Shirtwaist Factory, New York, NY	146
1946	Winecoff Hotel, Atlanta, GA	119

★ *Most are urban fires, not wildfires.*

Notes
★ More than 1.2 million acres of timberland destroyed
• 1.2 million acres burned
† 17,450 structures burned; $196 million of property loss

Historic U.S. Wildfires

- *October 8, 1871:* Michigan—200 fatalities, 2.5 million acres burned

- *September 4–6, 1881:* Lower Peninsula (Thumb area), Michigan—169 fatalities, about 1 million acres burned

- *August 20–21, 1910:* The Big Blowup; Washington, Idaho, and Montana—85 fatalities, 3 million acres burned

- *August 5, 1949:* Mann Gulch Fire, Helena National Forest, Montana—16 firefighters killed

- *November 1, 1966:* Loop Fire, Angeles National Forest, California—11 firefighters killed

- *Summer 1988:* Yellowstone National Park—nearly 800,000 acres burned

- *October 1991:* Oakland and Berkeley Hills, California—25 fatalities, more than 3,000 structures destroyed

- *November 2, 1993:* Malibu, California—3 fatalities

- *July 6, 1994:* Storm King Mountain, Colorado—14 firefighters killed

✳   ✳   ✳   ✳   ✳   ✳

Deadliest Fires in Recent History

Year	Location	Deaths
1845	Theater, Gangzhou, China	1,670
1871	Peshtigo, WI (forest fire)	1,182
1881	Ring Theater, Vienna, Austria	850
1903	Iroquois Theater, Chicago, IL	602
1994	Egypt (burning fuel flood)	500
1995	Schoolhouse, Dabwali, India	500
1942	Cocoanut Grove, Boston, MA	491
1913	Coal mine, Wales, England	439
1978	Movie theater, Abadan, Iran	425
1894	Hinckley, MN (forest fire)	418

LIFESAVING FACTS: HOW SHOULD YOU REACT?

Stop, drop, cover face, and roll! This is the number one rule for anyone whose clothes or body has caught fire. Serious injury or death can be prevented in other ways too.

Fire Safety Indoors and Out

• Never put anything over a lamp, like clothes or a blanket, not even when playing.

• Don't touch radiators or heaters unless you are certain how they work. If you aren't, ask an adult to help you.

• Don't stand too close to a fireplace or wood-stove. Your clothes might catch fire.

• Never play with matches, lighters, or candles. If you see matches or lighters where little children—or careless older ones—might find them, tell an adult.

• Turn off lights, stereos, TVs, and other electrical equipment when you are finished using them.

• Politely remind smokers to be careful with cigarettes.

• If you are camping, practice campfire safety:

> *Dig a pit away from overhanging branches.*
>
> *Circle it with rocks.*
>
> *Clear a five-foot area around the pit down to bare soil.*
>
> *Stack extra wood upwind and away from the fire.*
>
> *After lighting the campfire, do not discard the match until it is cold.*
>
> *Never leave a campfire unattended.*
>
> *Keep a bucket of water and a shovel nearby.*
>
> *Be sure your campfire is completely extinguished before you leave it.*

• Make sure your house has a smoke alarm on every floor—especially near bedrooms. Get help from an adult to check your smoke alarms once a month; replace batteries once a year. Familiarize younger kids with the loud beeping sound.

• Make sure your family has a working fire extinguisher.

• With your family plan fire escape routes, picking a safe place to meet outside. Try for two ways out of each room, in case one is blocked by fire. Practice a fire evacuation drill, crawling your family's escape routes at least once.

• If you see any sign of fire, report it to authorities immediately or tell a trustworthy adult.

In the Event of a Fire

• Before opening any door in a fire, feel it. If it's hot, fire may be on the other side. Try to get out another way.

• Crawl low through smoke.

• Escape and seek help; it's smarter and safer. Children should never try to fight fire.

• Once at your family's designated meeting place, see who's missing. Unnecessary searches endanger firefighters and others.

• Always get out and stay out. DO NOT go back for any possessions. If there's a person or pet still inside, tell a firefighter or other adult.

✯　　✯　　✯　　✯　　✯　　✯

Wildfire and Forest Fire Safety

The zone where residential areas expand into wildlands is an interface—a dangerous fire area. A dream home built in a wildland setting can be leveled by fire in minutes, especially because people build for rustic appearance to fit the wild setting. Almost every major wildland–urban interface fire in recent years has spread faster because of wood–shingle roofs. There are ways to reduce the risk:

- Create a thirty-foot low-fuel area, or safety zone, around the house. Thin out tree and brush cover. Remove dead limbs, fallen trees, leaves, twigs, and evergreen tree cones. Keep grass shorter than two inches. Prune branches ten feet up trunks to discourage ground fire from jumping to trees.

- Don't use highly flammable landscaping near structures. The best plants are high in water content and low in oil. Don't use bark or wood-chip mulch in the safety zone.

- If you live in a wildfire area, plan several escape routes by car and by foot. Include your pets if you can.

- Wildfires often move fast. If your family is told to evacuate, leave right away.

Thousands of brave men and women fight forest fires. Smoke jumpers parachute into isolated, rough, mountainous terrain to fight wildfires in hard-to-reach forest areas; it's important to get to the fire while it is still small. Smoke jumpers can drop into areas where there are no roads.

There are only 450 smoke jumpers in the world. These elite professionals come from all walks of life: Teachers, students, adventurists, and graduates in fields such as agriculture, geology, and forestry have all become jumpers. The work is seasonal, from April or June until September; most of the jumpers have winter jobs. There are several bases throughout the northwestern United States where jumpers live, ready if called. They work for the United States Forest Service or the Bureau of Land Management—though they all work together during busy years like 2000.

There are pilots who fly aircraft designed to drop water or fire retardants, either directly on the blaze or in a line to act as a firebreak. These pilots maneuver big aircraft down to nearly treetop level. It's been described as crop dusting with an airliner, only more dangerous. Pilots must coordinate closely with firefighters; a water or chemical drop made too close or from too low an altitude can injure or kill firefighters.

Helicopters are also used to combat fires. They can place large volumes of water at the right spot, even under difficult wildfire conditions. The pilots fly over the closest water source they can find, dipping huge buckets slung under the aircraft into the water, then fly back to dump water with pinpoint accuracy. Some firefighters rappel down ropes from helicopters to get to the flames.

"Mosquito" helicopters are set up with snorkels. The pilot hovers over a water source with the long snorkel hose hanging down. The flight crew pumps the belly tank full. A mosquito can use shallow ponds, reservoirs—even swimming pools.

A new type of fire-fighting helicopter was unveiled in 1998, the water cannon. One of the largest helicopters in the world, it looks like a cross between a science-fiction special effect and a squirt gun. Its 2,000-gallon water tank can be filled in forty-five seconds; it shoots a 300-gallon-per-minute stream of water or fire retardant 175 feet.

If the winds are favorable, backfires are set to rob the oncoming fire of the fuel it needs. In the 1988 fires that burned more than a third of Yellowstone

National Park, backfires saved parts of the park, convincing skeptics of their value. But it's always a risk. Backfires can become dangerous.

The Prescribed Burn

Firefighters sometimes use controlled fire to clear forests of debris. These friendly fires reduce undergrowth and help many plants reproduce; wildlife's food sources can even increase. But, most importantly, planned fires lessen the possibility of wildfire raging out of control.

Fire managers study the site and upcoming weather patterns to minimize the risk of fire escaping. They bulldoze firebreaks, or use existing ones, including roads, ditches, lakes, and so forth. On the day of the prescribed burn, if weather conditions are acceptable, fire crews light the fire with a drip torch. This is a fuel can with a flame-carrying torch-head spout. When the drip torch is tilted, fuel squirts, creating a stream of flame—sort of a low-pressure flamethrower.

Most prescribed fires are really two fires: a backfire and a head fire. Fire crews light a backfire downwind along the firebreak and let it slowly burn toward the site's center. Head fires are set so the wind carries flames toward the backfire. Most fire crew members work to contain the fire. Others put out small runaway flames. A nearby fire engine can be called in if the prescribed burn escalates into a wildfire. The recent "escaped" prescribed burn that ravaged huge areas of New Mexico's wildlands and threatened Los Alamos might just be a glaring example of what can happen if a burn isn't planned carefully.

Scientists hope satellites can help detect wildfires. The GOES-8 satellite orbits 22,300 miles above the equator. In 1995 researchers studying Brazil used a computer to analyze images and locate fire.

FRIGHTFULLY FUNNY AND SERIOUSLY STRANGE

When there is no escape from a fire, firefighters get under heat-reflective aluminized tents. Their slang for these personal survival shelters? "Shake and Bake." They also joke that they are waiting to see if they will be "crispy crittered."

Fire stations in some cities have poles the firefighters slide down, but in Arlington, Texas, most stations are one story high and don't need them. When an assistant fire chief built a house, he had his own fire pole installed. Arlington firefighters—and their wives and kids—must have a great sense of humor.

A six-thousand-acre wildfire near Grand Coulee, Washington, was started on August 6, 2000, by an unusual arsonist: a grasshopper. The insect encountered an electric cow-pasture fence. Investigators concluded that at least one big grasshopper struck the fence, caught fire, and fell into tall, dry grass.

An urban legend is a modern tall tale. People repeat it, claim it's true, often say it happened to "a friend of a friend." The following tale has been around since the 1980s. A Los Angeles radio station reported it as fact in 1997, but there's no real evidence. Like most urban legends, it's outlandish and funny:

> While checking the damage from a California forest fire, authorities found a corpse in a burned-out section of forest. The deceased male was dressed in a full wet suit, complete with an oxygen tank, flippers, and a face mask. A postmortem examination revealed that the man had died not from burns but from massive internal injuries. Dental records

were used to identify him. It turned out that on the day of the fire the man had been on a diving trip off the coast, twenty miles from the burning forest. The firefighters called in helicopters with large buckets—a technique used in many places. The huge buckets were dropped into the ocean for rapid filling, then flown to the forest fire and emptied. One minute the diver was swimming in the Pacific, the next he was doing a breaststroke in a fire bucket nine hundred feet in the air. A few minutes after that he was part of a water drop and apparently extinguished exactly five feet ten inches of the fire when he hit the ground.

chapter five

EARTHQUAKES

imagine this . . .

It is 1906, almost dawn on April 15. You are lying awake in a hotel bed, too excited to sleep another second. Two days ago your father brought the whole family into the city of San Francisco. It took all day in the carriage to get to Oakland, then another hour waiting for the ferry to come across the bay. When you finally got on board, your little sister was asleep in your mother's arms. She didn't waken as the ferry cast off, nor did the gentle motion of the waves disturb her in the least. You were glad. It was nice not to have her constant chattering as you stood beside your father watching the city come closer.

San Francisco looked so beautiful rising out of the sea, like some fairy city of brick and stone and mist. This journey has been a lifelong dream of your father's. The great opera singer Enrico Caruso performed last night, and you were there, spellbound, in the twentieth row. Even your little sister was silent and awestruck at the incredible soaring of the man's voice. When your father first started talking about this trip, the idea of hearing an opera singer had been less exciting to you than getting to come to the city of San Francisco—but the performance was as amazing as your father had promised it would be. And the fun isn't over yet. The weather has been wonderful and sunny, almost no fog at all, and your mother has talked your father into staying one more day so that you can all tour the city.

Now you just have to wait for everyone else to awaken so the wonderful day can begin. You close your eyes, then abruptly open them again. An odd groaning sound startles you into sitting straight up in bed. It goes on, getting louder. Then, before you can call out to your parents or react in any way, the hotel building shudders as though a giant has shoved it. You lurch out of bed, standing unsteadily, trying to keep your footing. The floor is rising and falling, a bizarre motion that should not be possible. The groaning is getting louder and louder, and you hear your sister cry out, then your mother scream. Your father shouts something you can't understand, then his voice shapes itself into a single word, "Earthquake!" Outside the open window you hear voices rising, jagged and sharp with fear, and the clatter of falling brick.

FREAKY (BUT TRUE!) FACTS

Ancient peoples believed a giant creature inside the earth caused earthquakes. Some cultures blamed a huge spider. Others attributed earthquakes to a colossal catfish, a hog, a whale, a turtle, or even a Godzilla-size dog scratching oversize fleas.

A legend in Assam (a state in northeastern India, between Bangladesh and China) teaches children that a race of underground people sometimes shake the ground to see if anyone still lives on the surface. When children in Assam feel a quake, they shout, "Alive! Alive!" so the people inside the earth will hear them and stop shaking.

More-scientific (but equally incorrect) theories have blamed earthquakes on the eruption of trapped underground wind or the collapse of underground caverns.

On August 17, 1999, a Richter magnitude 7.4 earthquake in Turkey killed 14,559 people and left 600,000 people homeless. The death toll was higher than it might have been because contractors had used substandard materials and building methods to cut costs. One contractor admitted mixing ordinary beach sand into concrete, instead of gravel. If the earthquake had come a week earlier, the death toll could have been even worse, because the country was packed with tourists (including the co-author of this book, Mary Barnes!) who had come to experience the August 11 total solar eclipse.

Enrico Caruso is considered by many to be the greatest operatic tenor of all time. He was on tour in San Francisco during the great earthquake of 1906, staying at the luxurious Palace Hotel. When he first felt his bed rocking, he thought he was dreaming about sailing home to Italy. Then he stumbled to the window to hear screams and to see buildings toppling and massive chunks of masonry crashing down. The legend (undocumented but interesting) is that he was afraid the earthquake terror might have damaged his voice, so he leaned out the window to sing a single magnificent note, startling people in the street below.

The earthquake that struck Lisbon, Portugal, in 1755 was felt as far as 1,400 miles away. People felt tremors in Portugal as well as Spain, North Africa, southern France, Italy, Switzerland, Scotland, Ireland, Germany, Holland, and Scandinavia.

The damage an earthquake does depends partly on how deep it is. The closer to the surface it is, the more damage it will cause.

✳   ✳   ✳   ✳   ✳   ✳

One week before the San Francisco Earthquake the Italian volcano Mount Vesuvius erupted. The people of San Francisco—soon to be accepting help from around the world themselves—collected $23,000 to send to the homeless victims in Italy.

The first shock of the magnitude 8.6 earthquake in Lisbon, Portugal, on All Saints' Day, November 1, 1755, caught 250,000 people at church. The second, stronger tremor collapsed buildings across the city, killing and trapping thousands. Huge quay-smashing tsunami waves battered the town. The ruins of the city burned for three days. It was a terrible triple disaster. Between 10,000 and 20,000 people died in Lisbon; 10,000 in neighboring Morocco.

During the fire that destroyed much of San Francisco following the 1906 earthquake, Union Square was packed with thousands of refugees. Trunks from a hotel were hauled there and unloaded in the square. Late that night the fire turned. The man guarding the trunks offered $1,000 for a team of horses to move them—a small fortune in 1906—but nobody was selling. The mountain of trunks were left to burn.

A 1923 Japanese earthquake destroyed a third of Tokyo and most of Yokohama. The massive shaking went on for five eternal minutes. Thousands of buildings crumbled, and a thirty-six-foot tsunami crashed against the coast. Then fires swept through. Tokyo holds annual commemoration services to honor survivors and casualties.

After the San Francisco Earthquake railroads gave more than a hundred thousand refugees free tickets to leave the city. Two women later said they had had to dress properly for train travel and couldn't flee the flames until they had put on straw hats with ribbons.

At the Yugoslav seaport of Bijela a 1979 earthquake snapped ten-story-high steel cranes and toppled them into the sea. A hundred-yard-long pier cracked and fell into the ocean.

After the 1906 San Francisco Earthquake people moved stoves out to the curb, and housewives did their cooking in the street—until all chimneys had been repaired and inspected for safety for the wood and coal fires used for cooking in those days.

During the last century:
• 1943 was the shakiest year, with forty-one magnitude 7 or higher earthquakes.
• 1986 was the quietest, with only six.
• 1976 marked the most earthquake deaths—295,000 to 699,000. The Tangshan Earthquake alone cost between 255,000 and 655,000 lives.

Earthquake survivors, freed after being buried in the dark for long periods, are often blindfolded before they emerge. Some people think it's to protect them from seeing the destruction; it's really to protect their eyes from the sudden sunlight.

In 1556 the people of Shaanxi Province in China carved their cave homes from cliffs. When an earthquake collapsed them, the death toll was an amazing and tragic 830,000.

In Kwantung, Japan, deep wells were lined with tile pipes. The 1923 earthquake shook the pipes out of the ground until they stood ten feet above the surface, like narrow tile chimneys.

After the 1906 San Francisco Quake people tried to save pianos from the fires by rolling them along the street. Piles of ashes full of tangled piano wires were seen after the fire.

People escaping from the fires following the San Francisco Earthquake tried hard to save precious belongings: A wealthy, well-known dry-goods merchant was seen nailing a pair of roller skates to the bottom of his trunk. Baby carriages were stacked with household treasures and dragged through the rubble-filled streets. People nailed together makeshift box-and-wheels carts; some carried hammers and nails to rebuild the carts when they fell apart on the debris-strewn streets. Horses were commandeered by the military, but family carriages were used to carry goods—with the whole family harnessed to pull them over the rough streets. Five people who had tied their goods to a long ladder used log-shaped rollers beneath it, pulling it forward about fifteen feet, then waiting for one woman to pick up the rollers and race around to lay them out ahead of the ladder again.

Many people piled belongings on caster-wheeled couches and pushed them along the sidewalks. Inventive people lashed boards between bicycle frames to create makeshift wagons; others were seen dragging chairs loaded with clothing and blankets.

The total energy released by earthquakes world-wide each year is about the same as the United States' annual energy consumption.

The 1959 Richter magnitude 7.5 earthquake that struck Hebgen Lake, Montana, caused a gigantic avalanche along the south wall of the Madison River canyon that filled the gorge with thirty-six million to forty-three million cubic yards of rock, soil, and trees. It blocked the Madison River. Within a few weeks a 175-foot-deep lake had formed.

The Richter magnitude 7.7 earthquake that struck Pleasant Valley, Nevada, on January 3, 1915, caused a mysterious increase in the flow of springs and streams throughout northern Nevada.

After San Francisco's 1906 earthquake a woman whose hip had been injured before the disaster was pushed through the rubble-clogged streets from near City Hall to the Oakland ferry on two bicycles lashed together by her sons. It took four days to get her to safety—she stayed on the makeshift bed the whole time.

One of the strongest U.S. earthquakes was Alaska's 1964 magnitude 9.2 Good Friday Earthquake. It lasted three minutes and killed 131 people, 122 of them victims of its tsunami. The town of Valdez was so damaged it cost $37.5 million to move it to a new site. The shaking raised the dock on Hinchinbrook Island, in Prince William Sound, by eight feet—making it useless except in extremely high tides. The earth under the village of Portage sank six feet; high tides flooded it. The new shoreline was two miles inland.

In 1811 and 1812 the largest known series of American earthquakes—near New Madrid, Missouri—changed the course of the Mississippi River.

After the 1906 San Francisco Earthquake the owner of a phonograph store found the first floor of his shop in a shambles; the second story, filled with thousands of phonograph records, was in perfect order, the shelves neat and orderly.

Seventy-five hours after the 1999 earthquake in Turkey, workers heard a voice coming from the rubble. A Hungarian rescue team with dogs was able to pinpoint the location. After five long hours of digging a three-year-old girl was pulled to safety.

On July 21, 1952, in Kern County, California, an earthquake cracked eighteen-inch reinforced concrete railroad tunnels—shortening one by eight inches. The rails were bent into S curves. Cotton rows were offset more than a foot, and a three-hundred-yard stretch of pavement was crumpled.

The epicenter of the 1923 Kwantung, Japan, earthquake was in Sagami Bay, which sank about 600 feet. At the same time, land at the north end of the bay was raised about 750 feet. Residents could not recognize their new hilly town site.

The 1906 San Francisco Earthquake caused the pavement in San Francisco to buckle, arch, and split. The shaking bent streetcar tracks into tortured curves. Fences and roads were relocated sideways four or five yards in some places. In Mendocino County a fence and a row of trees were displaced almost sixteen feet.

After the 1964 Alaskan Good Friday Earthquake the marquee of the Denali Theater in Anchorage was resting on the sidewalk. The sign hadn't fallen— the entire theater had sunk.

On Montague Island, Alaska, the land was raised thirty-three feet by the 1964 Good Friday Quake. Between the cliffs and the sea a quarter-mile-wide beach appeared. It is covered with a white coating of calcium, the remains of sea creatures that died when the quake lifted the land high and dry.

In 1923 an American tourist and his family were on opposite sides of a wide river when a Japanese earthquake hit. The man assumed the bridges would be down and made his way to the river mouth, intending to swim to his family. The earthquake had raised the river bottom almost six feet. He barely got his feet wet.

After the 1906 San Francisco Earthquake, U.S. soldiers patrolled to keep order, stop looting, and prevent more fires. A woman struck a match to light a Sterno can to heat milk for her baby. An officer ordered the flame put out and said he would have to shoot her if she did it again, because those were his orders.

A terrible earthquake on June 12, 1897, destroyed every building in a three-thousand-square-mile area of India. But the catastrophe left one beautiful gift behind: It tilted the land upward, giving a quiet little river a beautiful waterfall, which still flows.

In one house the 1906 San Francisco Earthquake flung bathwater to the ceiling. Pictures on the walls were neatly reversed, facing the wall.

Mima mounds are small, often regularly spaced bumps of soil and small stones one to six feet high. Scientists in North America, Africa, and South America have puzzled over their origin, favoring the idea that they are the work of pocket gophers. Then a geologist covered a sheet of plywood with sandy soil and jiggled it. Mounds formed at points where intersecting vibrations cancelled each other out—Mima mounds might be caused by earthquakes. In 1993, after a severe quake in India, formerly flat farmlands were topped by undulating mounds up to a foot high.

The 1897 earthquake in India flattened every brick or stone building in a 10,000-square-mile area. It damaged the town hall of Calcutta, 550 miles from the epicenter. The tremors were felt throughout almost 2,000,000 square miles.

The 1992 Landers quake in southern California was felt in high-rise buildings almost a thousand miles away, as far north as Boise, Idaho, and as far east as Denver, Colorado.

The earthquake in Kern County, California, on July 21, 1952, had far-reaching effects: Water splashed from swimming pools in Los Angeles, 100 miles away. Buildings there were damaged extensively, though most structures held. Water splashed in rooftop pressure tanks in San Francisco, 280 miles away. A building was damaged 230 miles away in San Diego.

The 1923 Kwantung, Japan, earthquake damaged a pottery shop. Fragile teapots, brightly decorated dishes, rice bowls, and saki cups stood weirdly unbroken under a nearly destroyed roof.

The 1959 magnitude 7.5 earthquake at Yellowstone National Park registered on seismographs in New Zealand and affected water levels in wells in Idaho, Hawaii, and Puerto Rico. In Las Vegas, Nevada, nearly three hundred miles away, a half-built building's structural steel had to be realigned after the shock.

In 1906 the luxurious Palace Hotel was San Francisco's grandest building, built to be earthquake proof and fireproof. Cement pillars buried twelve feet deep supported its foundation. Its brick walls were two feet thick, reinforced with three thousand tons of iron strips. The roof and basement had water storage tanks. There were five miles of water pipes, twenty thousand feet of fire hose, 350 faucets, and twelve fire hydrants. All eight hundred guest rooms had heat detectors. Employees and the fire department fought the great fire valiantly—but lost. The Palace Hotel burned.

Alaska's 1964 Good Friday Earthquake caused damage over a 50,000-square-mile area, was felt throughout 500,000 square miles, and caused the ground to rise or sink in a 100,000-square-mile area. Most of this was uninhabited land, but the quake damaged or destroyed hundreds of homes and businesses in downtown Anchorage, about 75 miles from the epicenter.

Missouri's New Madrid Earthquake in 1811 caused chimneys to fall in Cincinnati, 400 miles away. People were startled by shock waves in Boston, 1,100 miles away.

China's Great 1920 Earthquake did major damage throughout 15,000 square miles; tremors were felt within 1.5 million square miles.

Some kinds of wet, sandy soil, when shaken by earthquake tremors, lose frictional contact and behave like liquid. Buildings on this kind of soil are often completely destroyed. In late spring 1960 several Chilean earthquakes caused this kind of liquefaction. Almost five thousand square miles of coastline dropped about six feet. A parked car sank into the suddenly fluid soil. A river of liquefied sand flowed into the harbor at Puerto Montt, surrounding an anchored ship. When the sand settled, the ship was stuck. The owners turned it into a hotel.

Mexico City is built on an ancient lakebed. On September 19, 1985, a slab of the earth's crust beneath the Pacific Ocean forty miles offshore broke loose three hundred miles away from the city. It sent intense seismic waves that thundered beneath Mexico City and turned the sand and clay into vibrating jelly, causing extensive damage.

San Francisco's business district was hard hit by the 1906 earthquake; it was built on an unstable, filled-in cove. One man said Washington Street's brick surface rippled like ocean waves coming toward him. Another witness said the cobblestones "danced like corn in a popper." Valencia Street split open; people could hear a creek running under it. Nearby, another street burst open and a fountain of clear spring water sprayed skyward.

For three hours after the 1906 San Francisco Earthquake the outside world knew nothing of the disaster—telegraph wires were out. The Western Union Telegraph Company wire chief climbed poles, testing wires to find the break. Finally, during an eighteen-hour stint atop a thirty-foot pole, untangling wires and testing each one separately, he got a response from Sacramento. He sent the sad news, which was then relayed—stunning the world.

In the 1908 Messina, Italy, earthquake buildings were on unstable, sandy soil. Walls of river pebbles and bricks were mortared with sandy cement. Foundations shifted, unreinforced walls crumbled, heavy tile roofs collapsed.

All of Messina's police officials were killed or injured; eight hundred soldiers were trapped in collapsed barracks. Most prison inmates died when walls collapsed, but thirty violent convicts escaped and looted; they tried to rob the bank. When the Russian battleship *Admiral Makiroff* landed six hundred armed men, they routed the robbers and stood guard until Italian soldiers arrived.

Messina was rebuilt on its original site, but with a plan and strict building codes. The town is now believed to be "earthquake proof."

The 1923 earthquake in Kwantung, Japan, twisted and smashed a railroad bridge, displacing huge support piers. Amazingly, a footbridge made of two boards laid side by side was undamaged.

✗   ✗   ✗   ✗   ✗   ✗

After the December 7, 1988, Armenian earthquake a rescue worker saw a carton of eggs in the rubble. None were broken.

The captain of the *Argo,* a ship off the California coast in 1906, must have been amazed. The sea was calm, yet his ship started breaking up. Steel plates buckled, and bolts were blown out. Only later did he learn of the San Francisco Earthquake. The *Argo* must have been right over the fault when it happened.

Rescuers flown in after the September 19, 1985, Mexico City earthquake saw that many smaller buildings had been destroyed, while several skyscrapers were intact. The tall buildings had been designed to sway without collapsing.

An engineer pondered 1906 earthquake effects in San Francisco's Laurel Hill Cemetery. Two similar gravestones, fewer than two hundred feet apart, had shifted. One had turned right fifteen to twenty degrees; the other had turned to the left. A stone pedestal had turned; its decorative stone capital had turned the opposite direction.

✗   ✗   ✗   ✗   ✗   ✗

The September 19, 1985, Mexico City earthquake killed seven thousand people; it knocked out international telephone and telex lines. The eighteen million survivors were almost cut off from the world. Amateur radio operators passed on critical rescue information.

Messina, a few miles off the Italian coast, was a favorite European vacation spot in 1908, connected to the world by a few bad, winding roads, a seashore railway to the capital city, and an undersea telegraph cable to Reggio on the mainland. The 5:00 A.M. earthquake caused a tsunami that made Messina a jumble of ruins, along with Reggio on the mainland and dozens of villages. Between 70,000 and 100,000 people died. The quake snapped telegraph cable, destroyed rails and bridges, and left roads impassable except on foot. Hours later a dazed, half-naked victim staggered into a neighboring village with the tragic news.

On October 17, 1989, Candlestick Park in Loma Prieta, California, was packed with more than 62,000 fans watching the third game of the World Series. At 5:04 P.M. a Richter magnitude 7.1 earthquake struck, lasting twenty seconds. Then came two and a half minutes of shocked silence citywide—then a magnitude 5.2 aftershock. The World Series Quake killed 63 people, injured 3,757, left more than 12,000 people homeless, and caused $10 billion in damage.

An ancient citadel in Hercegnovi, Yugoslavia, withstood attacks by foreign armies for more than five hundred years but fell into the sea during a 1979 earthquake.

If a 1925 earthquake in Montana had occurred sixty seconds earlier, it would have buried a transcontinental train and its passengers under a huge landslide.

The 1964 Prince William Sound earthquake devastated schools in Anchorage, Alaska. The Government Hill Grade School, sitting atop a huge landslide, was torn apart. The south wing dropped thirty feet. The east wing split lengthwise and collapsed. No one was hurt because schools were closed for Good Friday.

Massive waves swept across Hebgen Lake for *twelve hours* after the earthquake on August 17, 1959, in Yellowstone National Park.

The 1923 Kwantung, Japan, earthquake caused a mudflow two hundred yards wide and fifty feet deep that picked up an entire train and carried it into the bay, killing more than two hundred people.

On March 10, 1933, a Richter magnitude 6.3 earthquake in Long Beach, California, destroyed empty school buildings. Hours earlier, when classrooms were full, ten thousand to thirty thousand schoolchildren could have died. Weeks later the state legislature passed a law to make new schools earthquake safe.

A 1960 earthquake in Agadir, Morocco, affected a small area and lasted only six seconds. For five of those seconds people heard a weird groaning sound. During the sixth second,the ground beneath the town shifted four feet, then snapped back. The quake killed 10,000 to 15,000 people, injured another 25,000, and destroyed 70 percent of new buildings and 20 percent of industrial buildings. Nobody was willing to rebuild, so the area was abandoned.

✕　　✕　　✕　　✕　　✕　　✕

A county geologist in Santa Clara, California, kept a relic of the 1906 San Francisco Earthquake— a rare glass photographic plate showing the demolished City Hall, on which hung a sign asking in large letters, WHY? The fragile memento survived until 1989. The World Series Quake shattered it.

The Richter 7.8 Mexico City earthquake in 1985 hit at rush hour, shaking the city for nearly two minutes. Buildings tumbled, fires broke out, and electrical lines snapped. Subways and trolleys stopped; traffic lights failed. Hundreds of thousands of people ran into the streets. It was instant, insane gridlock.

The 1923 Kwantung, Japan, earthquake threw potatoes out of the ground and left them lying scattered across the field.

Earthquakes usually tear down bridges, but the 1923 Kwantung, Japan, earthquake *unearthed* the pilings of a seven-hundred-year-old bridge.

After the September 19, 1985, Mexico City earthquake it began to rain. Hundreds of thousands were homeless—or afraid to go in their cracked and unstable houses. In parks and streets makeshift tent communities made of plastic, pieces of wood furniture, and donated blankets sprang up. One encampment ran a TV wire up an electrical pole to get a set running. There was no real shelter, food, or water, but there was televised soccer.

On January 17, 1995, an earthquake near Japan's most important port, Kobe, collapsed many twenty-year-old high-rise buildings at the fifth floor. The building code back then allowed a weaker super-structure beginning at the fifth floor.

On December 16, 1920, in Gansu Province, China, there had not been an earthquake in 280 years. Then the magnitude 8.6 Great 1920 Earthquake struck. Villagers died when landslides, or "hills that walked," covered their villages. People in ten cities perished when shock waves tore stone buildings apart. In the days that followed twenty thousand earthquake survivors froze to death for lack of shelter—in all, two hundred thousand died.

Most deaths in the World Series Quake were caused when a mile-long elevated section of Interstate 880 in Oakland collapsed. The death toll could have been higher. Many people had left work early to see the third game on TV.

In the early 1500s Spanish conquistadores wiped out nearly 90 percent of Guatemalan natives. They brought a building style that would kill another 23,000 Guatemalans in the twentieth century. Picturesque adobe houses with heavy tile roofs were no match for the magnitude 7.5 earthquake that struck on February 4, 1976.

Animal Earthquake Detectors?

After the September 19, 1985, Mexico City quake a search-and-rescue-dog handler noticed her dog's ears were up. The fur on his back rose, and he circled uneasily. Nearly three minutes later an aftershock struck. Later, searching a parking garage under an office complex, her dog acted the same way. Together they raced toward the exit, a faint rumbling vibrating the air around them. Just as they emerged into the street, the building collapsed into the parking garage in an explosive roar.

In 1990 a graduate student working in the University of Southern California's Learning and Memory Laboratory watched three caged rabbits sitting calmly. For no reason he could discern, they abruptly started thrashing wildly in their cages and continued for about five minutes. Then a Richter magnitude 5.2 earthquake rocked the building.

Japanese fishermen have reported catching deep-sea fish near the surface just prior to earthquakes.

There are stories of deer coming out of the woods and mingling with humans without fear just before earthquakes.

On February 4, 1975, odd animal behavior prompted Chinese officials to evacuate the city of Haicheng. Several hours later a magnitude 7.3 earthquake destroyed 90 percent of the city. The evacuation saved nearly ninety thousand lives. China has been hit without warning by several major quakes, and there have also been false alarms from unusual animal behavior. But still, if animals can sense something before earthquakes, people need to figure out what.

AMERICA'S MOST FAMOUS: THE SAN FRANCISCO EARTHQUAKE

A magnitude 7.7 earthquake struck San Francisco, California, at daybreak on April 18, 1906. It was felt all over California and in parts of Nevada and Oregon. The shocks were like ocean waves and lasted a full minute.

Along the quake's center, the San Andreas Fault, the tall brick and stone buildings in the financial district, the San Francisco Mint, world-famous hotels, boardinghouses, bakeries, businesses, and homes were damaged or destroyed. Trees were uprooted, steel trolley tracks were twisted, and water pipes were broken, cutting off the city's water supply.

Across the city coals from parlor fires were rattled from the hearth onto the rug. In bakeries glowing embers from shattered baking ovens were thrown onto wooden floors, skidding into lard tins and flour barrels. Outside, broken electrical wires snaked wildly, flashing blue sparks. The streets arched and fell, buckling the cobblestone surface. The earth itself was piled into ridges as broken pipes sprayed water into the dust-clogged air.

Within minutes the streets were full of weeping, giddy people. Within an hour it was obvious the small fires that had started across the city would soon engulf it. San Francisco's experienced firemen reported to work all over the city, but the broken pipes meant there was no water to douse the fires.

Within hours the streets were crammed with desperate people.

An emergency military takeover limited looting and drinking—but it also meant that all automobiles and horses were commandeered for official use. People carried their most precious possessions. One man said he saw more "talking machines" (phonographs—a new and expensive invention) in that one day than he had in his lifetime. One woman carried ironing boards and an iron. Another had a new broom in one hand and a large black hat with ostrich plumes in the other. A young lady on a bicycle carried a suit box under one arm, a canary cage dangling from the handlebars. An elderly woman carried a birdcage with four kittens inside, while the parrot perched on her hand. Many people had filled heavy steamer trunks with their treasures.

Novelist Jack London described the awful scene:

> They held on longest to their trunks, and over these trunks many a strong man broke his heart that night. The hills of San Francisco are steep, and up these hills, mile after mile, were the trunks dragged. Everywhere were trunks with across them lying their exhausted owners, men and women.

Before the march of the flames were flung picket lines of soldiers. . . . One of their tasks was to keep the trunk-pullers moving. The exhausted creatures, stirred on by the menace of bayonets, would arise and struggle up the steep pavements, pausing from weakness every five or ten feet. Often, after surmounting a heart-breaking hill, they would find another wall of flame advancing upon them at right angles and be compelled to change anew the line of their retreat.

WEIRD TALES OF SURVIVAL

People who are not rescued from earthquake-collapsed buildings within forty-eight hours have only about a 10 percent chance of surviving. But some do, and in the strangest ways. Five days after an earthquake devastated Taiwan in September 1999, two brothers were pulled alive from the rubble of a Taipei building. They had kept their spirits up by talking and fought starvation by eating rotten apples from a refrigerator that was buried with them.

During an earthquake on August 17, 1999, the bed of a sleeping Turkish couple plunged downward into a kitchen three floors below. One end of the bed frame caught on a kitchen counter and created a tiny haven that protected them until, forty hours later, they felt a rush of fresh air and a rescuer's hand.

In the September 19, 1985, Mexico City earthquake the first floor of a block-long, eleven-story clothing factory dropped completely into the basement, leaving the second floor at street level. The top four floors pancaked down onto the seven below, leaving layers of debris. Thirty-five female garment workers escaped, but fifty-nine were trapped in the flattened upper rooms; friends and relatives heard their cries, but the heavy equipment needed to free them was assigned to other areas. The voices had faded, but were still sometimes heard, when rescue workers decided the building was too unstable, too dangerous, and left.

The owners allowed a few workers into the shattered ground floor to salvage office equipment and clothing, but kept the workers' husbands and brothers away for fear of disastrous amateur rescue attempts. After nearly a week, in the chaos of citywide repair efforts, the building was scheduled to be bulldozed; it was endangering buildings around it. At 2:00 A.M. a relative of one of the trapped women begged American rescue-dog handlers to help. He said they could still hear voices, but because the trapped women were poor, no one cared.

Handlers and their dogs crawled into the factory's second floor, now at ground level. The dogs led the way up a debris slide to the third floor. One dog leaped, barking at the ceiling. That meant there was life above, but where and how much higher in the dangerous wreckage? Handlers worked in pairs, the second acting as observer. Rats skittered in the darkness, their eyes red in the flashlight beams.

Another handler went to the fourth floor. Her dog, Aly, led her into the debris and disappeared into a small opening. The handler inched forward on her stomach. In her flashlight beam she saw her dog a dozen feet ahead, digging and whining. When he saw her, he barked and bounded back. Accustomed to being rewarded with a stick to play with when he found someone alive, he grabbed her flashlight and raced back through the black tunnel to announce his success to the following observer. Without light, the rescuer reached a wall of debris. Then her dog came back with her flashlight.

The rescuer slowly figured out that two young seamstresses were trapped by debris and dead bodies on the sixth floor, near a broken window. They had managed to drink a little rainwater but were near death when they heard Aly barking. A rescue team brought a crane, rappelled down the side of the building from the roof, and entered through a window on the crushed sixth floor. A medic brought water and started intravenous drips to rehydrate the weak survivors. It took twelve more hours of careful work to free the women without bringing the building down. The rescue dogs and their handlers were, as they are so often, heroes.

Eighteen days after the 1908 Messina, Italy, earthquake two girls and their baby brother were found in a cellar, where they had survived on raw vegetables and olive oil.

Five days after the December 7, 1988, Armenian earthquake rescue dogs insistently signaled their handlers that someone was under a collapsed building—badly injured but alive. Firemen from America's Virginia and Florida rescue teams slowly and carefully worked downward through the unstable debris, shoring up a tunnel as they went. Five hours later they found a woman who had been saved by a refrigerator. It had tipped over at an angle, shielding her and creating an air pocket. She was semiconscious, barely able to breathe—a dead body's leg was pressed against her throat by tons of debris overhead. A trauma surgeon from Illinois was held suspended above the woman while he amputated the lifeless limb. As he finished he accidentally kicked a jack supporting the wreckage. Firemen lifted the woman up through the tunnel and everyone hurried out of the shaking rubble. They escaped just before it thundered down in a cloud of cement dust.

An aftershock of the 1988 Armenian earthquake trapped a handler and her dog who were searching rubble. It was pitch-black; her flashlight was gone. As she radioed for help her dog disappeared, then came back, sounding a "Follow me!" bark. He led his grateful handler through a twisting maze of rubble to a second-story balcony, now just above the street.

Just before the 1906 San Francisco Earthquake a widowed mother left her two-year-old daughter, Annie, sleeping while she went to the produce market. She raced home to find her house demolished. She dug frantically through rubble until neighbors made her stop; they said Annie couldn't have survived. The woman wandered the streets, showing people a picture of Annie. After two days a policeman told her some children had been ferried to Oakland. She continued her search.

More than fifty thousand refugees were camped in Oakland. The mother walked ceaselessly, showing the picture without luck. Finally, after dark, she found a man and his wife sitting in front of a tent, breaking bread into a pot of stew. She showed them the picture. Without a word the man got up, went into the tent, and returned carrying Annie. He had rescued her. Not seeing a parent, he had taken her to safety with his wife and children.

The night of the 1908 Messina, Italy, earthquake the Trinacria Hotel was packed with foreign business visitors. A London ship owner named Dorsey was on the top floor. The next room held Charles Caiger, an English ship architect, and next to him was a Swedish couple with a baby. Awakened by shaking, crashing, and screaming, they all made their way to Caiger's room, then, terrified by the calamity, waited in the darkness. Dawn revealed that nothing was left of the hotel except for their three rooms. It had *completely* collapsed, right up to their very walls. They made a long rope from sheets and blankets. The father bound his baby across his chest and led the way down. Struggling through debris and dead bodies, they reached the ruined dock, where a British steamer took them to safety.

After the Messina earthquake Russian sailors rescued 110 injured survivors. With the walls still trembling from aftershocks, they scaled a demolished building to rescue a woman who had clung thirty feet above the ground for almost twelve hours.

British sailors heard a voice calling, "Maria! Maria!" They dug through debris and found a dark cellar. A rescuer struck a match and laughed. A big green parrot was crying, "Maria! Maria!" He picked up the bird, then wondered if it was calling to someone. Behind a jammed door he found an unconscious girl. She and her parrot recovered.

Before Messina's ruined walls were dynamited, an Italian soldier dreamed his "dead" fiancée had called to him. A skeptical officer let him search; she was dug from her basement, slightly injured.

More than two weeks after the Messina earthquake a weak three-year-old boy was found alive— under his parents' bodies.

Almost eighty days after the devastating September 1999 Taiwan earthquake, workers preparing to demolish a collapsed house discovered a cat pinned down by furniture in the debris. The severely dehydrated animal was barely breathing and weighed only five pounds—half what it should have. It had survived by eating a nearby dead cat but was comatose after more than *two months* of being trapped. A TV reporter took it to a vet.

TALL TALES AND DANGEROUS MYTHS

Earthquake tales describe huge cracks in the earth opening up and swallowing people, or even whole towns, then closing back over them without a trace. It never happens, except in movies.

Some people have claimed to see fire erupting from the earth during an earthquake, but there is no scientific evidence of that ever happening.

Is there "earthquake weather"? Every region of the world has a story about it—but the definition changes to whatever weather was going on in the region when the last major quake hit.

A common myth is that big earthquakes happen in the early morning, but they can happen any time of the day or night.

✗   ✗   ✗   ✗   ✗   ✗

Many people have seen pictures of collapsed adobe homes with just the doorway left standing. That has led to the belief that during an earthquake the safest place in a building is a doorway. And that is true—if you are in an old, unreinforced adobe house.

HOW BAD WAS IT: SCALES AND MEASURES

The first known instrument for measuring earthquakes was invented in A.D. 132 by Chang Heng, the imperial astronomer of China. His earthquake weathercock was a copper kettle, six feet across, decorated with birds, animals, and mountains. The top was circled by eight dragon heads, each one holding a bronze ball in its mouth. Under each dragon was a bronze toad, its mouth wide open to catch the falling ball. When an earthquake struck, the shaking would ring a bell and jiggle a ball from its dragon's-mouth perch into the mouth of the bronze frog below it. The ball that fell would indicate the direction of the earthquake.

It was an amazing creation, but six years after its invention it seemed to have malfunctioned. The bell rang and a ball dropped into a frog's mouth—but no one had felt anything! Days later an exhausted messenger brought news of an earthquake four hundred miles northwest! After that, earthquake victims in distant provinces no longer had to summon aid. When a ball fell, authorities sent a rescue expedition in that direction.

Today scientists measure earthquakes in two ways. The first is to measure the energy released by an earthquake's movement using one of the thousands of seismographic stations worldwide. That measurement is called the quake's magnitude.

A seismograph works like a pendulum dangling from a string attached to a frame. During an earthquake it looks like the pendulum is shaking, but it's really remaining still while the instrument's base shakes along with the earth. It traces the movement on a strip of graph paper that moves past it on a revolving drum.

The scale of magnitude most people are familiar with is the Richter scale. On the Richter scale every whole number on the scale represents ten times the energy of the number below it. For instance, magnitude 8 is ten times stronger than magnitude 7, and a hundred times stronger than magnitude 6 (multiply 10 x 10). So a magnitude 8 earthquake isn't twice as powerful as a magnitude 4, it is ten thousand times as strong (multiply 10 x 10 x 10 x 10).

✳   ✳   ✳   ✳   ✳   ✳

The chart below describes the typical effects of earthquakes of various Richter magnitudes.

Magnitude	Effects
Less than 3.5	Generally not felt, but recorded
3.5–5.4	Often felt, but rarely causes damage
Under 6.0	At most, slight damage to well-designed buildings; can cause major damage to poorly constructed buildings over small regions
6.1–6.9	Can be destructive in residential areas up to 100 kilometers across
7.0–7.9	Major earthquake; can cause serious damage over larger areas
8 or greater	Great earthquake; can cause serious damage in areas several hundred kilometers across.

Magnitude can also be expressed as surface-wave magnitude, which measures the size of the seismic waves crackling around Earth's surface. The newest and most accurate way to describe magnitude is through moment magnitude. This is based on the size of an earthquake's fault and how much the earth actually slips.

A second kind of earthquake measurement is based upon how much an earthquake is felt and how much damage it does. This is the earthquake's intensity, usually based on observations of survivors. The observations are ranked on the modified Mercalli scale, which is divided into twelve parts, each designated by a Roman numeral. The scale starts at imperceptible shaking and goes all the way up to catastrophic destruction. Although intensity is more subjective and less scientific than magnitude, it allows scientists to estimate the size of earthquakes without any instruments, based on sources like newspapers and diaries.

The Modified Mercalli Scale

I. People do not feel any Earth movement.

II. A few people might notice movement if they are at rest and/or on the upper floors of tall buildings.

III. Many people indoors feel movement. Hanging objects swing back and forth. People outdoors might not realize that an earthquake is occurring.

IV. Most people indoors feel movement. Hanging objects swing. Dishes, windows, and doors rattle. The earthquake feels like a heavy truck hitting the walls. A few people outdoors may feel movement. Parked cars rock.

V. Almost everyone feels movement. Sleeping people are awakened. Doors swing open or closed. Dishes are broken. Pictures on the wall move. Small objects move or are turned over. Trees might shake. Liquids might spill out of open containers.

VI. Everyone feels movement. People have trouble walking. Objects fall from shelves. Pictures fall off walls. Furniture moves. Plaster in walls might crack. Trees and bushes shake. Damage is slight in poorly built buildings. No structural damage.

VII. People have difficulty standing. Drivers feel cars shaking. Some furniture breaks. Loose bricks fall. Damage is slight to moderate in well-built buildings, considerable in poorly built buildings.

VIII. Drivers have trouble steering. Houses not bolted down might shift on their foundation. Tall structures, like towers and chimneys, might twist and fall. Well-built buildings suffer slight damage. Poorly built structures suffer severe damage. Tree branches break. Hillsides might crack if the ground is wet. Water levels in wells might change.

IX. Well-built buildings suffer considerable damage.

Houses not bolted down move off their foundation. Some underground pipes are broken. The ground cracks. Reservoirs suffer serious damage.

X. Most buildings and their foundations are destroyed. Some bridges are destroyed. Dams are seriously damaged. Large landslides occur. Water sloshes out of canals, rivers, lakes. The ground cracks in large areas. Railroad tracks bend slightly.

XI. Most buildings collapse. Some bridges are destroyed. Large cracks appear in the ground. Underground pipelines are destroyed. Railroad tracks are badly bent.

XII. Almost everything is destroyed. Objects are thrown into the air. The ground moves in waves or ripples. Large amounts of rock may move.

WHY, HOW, AND WHERE CAN IT HAPPEN?

Earth's crust is divided up into huge tectonic plates that fit together like 3-D puzzle pieces forming our globe-shaped planet. These plates are always moving. When they slip or grind past each other, the earth can shake with the release of tension or energy. We call this an earthquake.

Earthquakes are usually mild. We might hear a

low, rumbling noise, notice the ground shaking gently, or feel a sharp jolt. Hanging plants might swing back and forth, shelved dishes and knick-knacks might jiggle. In a few earthquakes the shaking is strong enough to cause enormous damage.

More than 90 percent of earthquakes occur on fractures and cracks along the boundaries of the tectonic plates. These fractures are called faults. A fault line is marked by rocks on either side of a fracture that have moved in opposite directions, either vertically, horizontally, or at an angle. A fault line can be several inches or thousands of miles long.

There are three main types of faults. When two plates are moving away from each other, a *divergent fault* results. A *convergent fault* occurs when two plates press together. When two plates slide horizontally past each other, the result is a *transform fault*.

The movement of rock along a fault is not smooth and continuous. Instead, pressure builds up as the two sides push at each other. At first, friction keeps them from moving. When the pressure is enough to overcome the friction, the rocks slip suddenly and sometimes violently. The built-up energy between the two sides is released and travels outward through the rock in waves, the same way pond ripples spread.

The motion starts at a point deep down in the fault, called the hypocenter. The point on the surface of the earth directly above the hypocenter is the epicenter, where we say the earthquake "occurred."

The famous San Andreas Fault runs north-south for 650 miles through California. It is a transform fault; the tectonic plate on the west side of the San Andreas is the Pacific Plate, which covers most of the Pacific Ocean floor and California's coastline. On the east side is the North American Plate, which covers most of the continent and parts of the Atlantic Ocean floor.

It is a popular myth that the coast of California will break off and sink into the Pacific Ocean. But most of the movement along the San Andreas is horizontal, not vertical. The west side of the fault is moving northward at about two inches a year; about as fast as fingernails grow. In a mere twenty million years San Francisco will be where Seattle now is. All along the San Andreas Fault offset streams, sometimes displaced by half a mile or more, show where the plates have moved horizontally.

Most earthquakes occur around the rim of the Pacific Ocean, known as the Ring of Fire. A large earthquake has never been recorded in Australia, because it isn't close to any tectonic plate boundaries.

HOW OFTEN DO EARTHQUAKES HAPPEN?

Near Hollister, California, the Calaveras Fault creeps along steadily at about half an inch a year and causes twenty thousand tiny earthquakes a year, most of them too small to feel. Elsewhere faults fit together tightly, resisting slippage for hundreds of years. The longer the interval, the more strain that builds up, and the stronger the earthquake will be.

It's easy to predict earthquakes. Will there be one today? Yes. The answer is always yes. In the time it takes you to read this page an earthquake or two will happen somewhere in the world—they occur about every thirty seconds! On average, a year of earthquakes breaks down like this:

Magnitude	Number of Earthquakes
8	1 per year
7–8	18 per year
6–7	120 per year
5–6	800 per year
4–5	6,200 per year
3–4	49,000 per year
< 3	9,000 per day!!

If you are ever bored during an earthquake—after you have crawled under a sturdy table or run to open ground—try to estimate the distance to the epicenter. Earthquakes produce two types of waves that travel at different speeds; the more time between them, the farther away the epicenter is. The P wave comes first, quick and jolting. Then comes the slower, rolling S wave. After the P wave hits, count the seconds until you feel the S wave, then multiply by five. This gives you the distance in miles to the epicenter. If the earthquake is far enough away, you won't feel the jolt of the P wave at all; it weakens with distance.

THE EARTHQUAKE HALL OF FAME

Many quakes happened before human record keeping began. Chile's 1960 magnitude 9.5 quake was the first that size to be scientifically measured. The United States Geological Survey lists these fifteen largest earthquakes in the United States:

Location	Year	Magnitude
Prince William Sound, AK	1964	9.2
Andreanof Islands, AK	1957	8.8
Rat Islands, AK	1965	8.7

East of Shumagin Islands, AK	1938	8.3
Lituya Bay, AK	1958	8.3
Yakutat Bay, AK	1899	8.2
Near Cape Yakataga, AK	1899	8.2
Andreanof Islands, AK	1986	8.0
New Madrid, MO	1812	7.9
Fort Tejon, CA	1857	7.9
Kau District, HI	1868	7.9
Kodiak Island, AK	1900	7.9
Gulf of Alaska	1987	7.9
Owens Valley, CA	1872	7.8
Imperial Valley, CA	1892	7.8

Here are the fifteen largest earthquakes in the contiguous United States:

Location	Year	Magnitude
New Madrid, MO	1812	7.9
Fort Tejon, CA	1857	7.9
Owens Valley, CA	1872	7.8
Imperial Valley, CA	1892	7.8
New Madrid, MO	1811	7.7
San Francisco, CA	1906	7.7
Pleasant Valley, NV	1915	7.7

Landers, CA	1992	7.6
New Madrid, MO	1812	7.6
Kern County, CA	1952	7.5
Hebgen Lake, MT	1959	7.5
West of Lompoc, CA	1927	7.3
Dixie Valley, NV	1954	7.3
Borah Peak, ID	1983	7.3
West of Eureka, CA	1922	7.3

These are the top ten deadliest earthquakes in the history of the world, listed in order of greatest number of deaths:

Location	Year	Deaths	Magnitude
Shaanxi, China	1556	830,000	Unknown
Calcutta, India	1737	300,000	Unknown
Tangshan, China	1976	255,000	8.0
Aleppo, Syria	1138	230,000	Unknown
Near Xining, China	1927	200,000	8.3
Damghan, Iran	856	200,000	Unknown
Gansu, China	1920	200,000	8.6
Ardabil, Iran	893	150,000	Unknown
Kwantung, Japan	1923	143,000	8.3
Hebei, China	1290	100,000	Unknown
Messina, Italy	190	70,000–100,000	7.5

Before

- Bolt or strap cupboards and bookcases to the walls and keep heavy objects on the lower shelves so they don't fall on people.

- Strap your water heater to a nearby wall. This will keep it from falling on someone or starting a fire from a broken gas pipe or live wires.

- Have your home bolted to the foundation. Anchor bolts cost as little as two dollars each. They should be installed every six feet on the outer edges of your house.

- Take these precautionary measures with other home hazards:

  China cabinet: Attach it to wall studs.

  Tall knickknack shelves: Attach them to wall studs.

  Bookshelves: Attach them to wall studs.

  Heavy hanging plants: Use light, unbreakable pots; hang them from ceiling studs.

  Wall mirror: Make sure it is well fastened.

  Unsecured TV on a rolling cart: Block wheels.

  Bed by a big window: Move it away.

  Heavy picture above a bed: Move bed or picture.

  Hanging light above a bed: Secure light with wire or chain.

Cabinet doors not fastened to stay closed:
Install latches.

Gas stove's rigid feed line: Replace it with flexible line.

Heavy wall clock: Attach it to wall studs.

Flammable liquids and other toxins: Store them on bottom shelves.

Chimney: Brace it to the house outside.

During

• Drop and cover. This means drop to the floor and get *under* something for cover. At the first indication of the ground shaking, immediately take cover under a heavy desk or table, or other heavy object.

• If you can't get under cover, lying down next to a strong piece of furniture might save you. When buildings collapse, strongly built furniture may create open areas, or voids, within the mass of debris. In fact, some rescue experts insist you are safer lying next to your desk than under it, where you might get crushed if it collapses.

• If there is no desk or table to provide cover, face an inside wall away from glass surfaces. Kneel close to it and cover your head with your hands and arms. In an auditorium or theater crouch on the floor between chairs and cover your head.

• If inside a modern, well-built building, stay inside. Outside other buildings or outer walls could fall on you.

• If outside, move away from big buildings, structures, overhead power lines, gas lines, elevated expressways, or anything that could fall on you. Lie down or crouch low to the ground.

• If you are in a moving car, stop but stay in the car. Don't stop near or under overpasses, buildings (in a parking garage, for example), or utility wires.

After

• If you smell gas, open a window.
• Extinguish small fires.
• Get your emergency kit and leave the building.
• Never use elevators; the power will probably go off.
• Move to an open area away from buildings and power and gas lines.
• If driving a car, watch for broken roads, fallen bridges, and other hazards.

✷   ✷   ✷   ✷   ✷   ✷

TERROR TECHS, WEATHER WIZARDS, AND DISASTER DOCTORS

No one can prevent earthquakes. Scientists are trying to learn to predict them. Early warning can minimize damage and loss of life. Architects are learning how to design buildings—even skyscrapers—that sway or rock harmlessly on giant rollers.

In Parkfield, California, there is a magnitude 6.0 earthquake about every twenty-two years. Researchers have installed an array of sensitive equipment there to try to detect phenomena that might give warning of an impending quake. In Kobe, Japan, scientists are trying to learn whether rocks under stress emit unusual electromagnetic signals in the weeks before a quake. Geologists called paleoseismologists search for earthquakes from the past. They dig deep trenches in seismically active areas and study the earth's layers of soil and rock to determine how much time passed between major earthquakes in that area.

Rescue experts are constantly developing new ways to help earthquake victims. Seismic sound teams and remote TV crews use devices dropped by cable through layers of fallen concrete slabs to detect the breathing—even the heartbeat—of trapped victims. Low-light miniature TV cameras can be snaked by fiber-optic cable through cracks and crevices, recording human shapes and movement hidden by hundreds of feet of wreckage. These tiny cameras can also help find the safest way to pull away debris.

Four-Footed Heroes

Confusion reigns in the days following terrible earthquakes as separated family members try to find one another. Trained expert rescuers search for survivors in the rubble. Some of them have paws.

Search-and-rescue dogs, taught to find the scent of humans under the wreckage, pick their way carefully over shaky piles of sharp debris. They are often fitted with sturdy booties to protect their feet.

On crowded rescue sites search-and-rescue dogs are able to ignore the odors of the rescue people and search for new human scents that might be buried in the debris. By gauging their dogs' reactions, handlers can tell whether a live person or a dead one has been found. A live find will prompt barking, tail wagging, pricked ears, and eager scratching at a spot. With a body find a dog might signal by flattening its ears and tucking its tail between its hind legs—some have fur rise along their back. Other dogs react to the smell of death by instinctively marking the spot with urine. Still others start quickly backpedaling.

These responses are not taught to the dogs. Each has its own. It's the handlers' job to learn to translate what their canine partners are telling them. The dogs are rewarded with a play stick and lavish praise, but they seem to take pride and pleasure in saving lives apart from the rewards.

In Mexico City's quake aftermath the dogs found mostly dead bodies for two long days. The American handlers noticed they were dragging along, refusing to eat, reluctant to work. A Mexican veterinarian hid under the wreckage of the next day's site. One by one, the search dogs went in, picked up his scent, and found him. The dogs' spirits rose, and they went back to work.

Humans' noses have about 5 million smell receptor cells; dogs' noses have more than 220 million. Their brains process odor information differently too. A dog's sensitivity to certain molecules may be thousands of times greater than a human's.

FRIGHTFULLY FUNNY AND SERIOUSLY STRANGE

During rescue efforts after the Mexico City earthquake video monitors showed the lowered fiber-optic camera had reached an obstacle and couldn't move any farther. Suddenly the on-screen blob opened and became a woman's eye. The light of the camera must have made her blink.

In another case the high-tech cable was used to lower water to a couple trapped far below in collapsed debris. It might well have been the world's most expensive rope.

During the 1906 San Francisco Earthquake the front of a third-floor hotel room had fallen into the street, carrying with it some clothes on a chair. The owner called down to a workman and offered him twenty dollars to bring the suit back up to his room. The workman agreed, but just then an aftershock struck. "Ah," the workman said, reconsidering the price of his own life, "you better come and get it yourself."

Alone in her Mexico City hotel room after the 1985 quake, a U.S. volunteer rescue-dog handler noticed a crack in the wall above her bed, then a three-foot hole in the ceiling. An earlier shock had loosened a ceiling light fixture that had fallen, bringing plaster down with it. The opening was now covered by carpet in the room above. Returning from her first day of searching, she saw that the crack over the bed had lengthened several inches. Staring upward uneasily, she was startled when the carpet was pulled aside and a man's face appeared. He introduced himself as one of two Scandinavian reporters occupying the room above. After a brief chat he covered the hole again.

A radio station in the San Francisco Bay area reported one morning that a sequence of eight small quakes had shaken the area. The first was at about 6:30, the next at about 6:45, and the third at about 6:55. A caller to the station said, "Hey, how about that! An earthquake with a snooze alarm!"

In Hollywood there is a large digital billboard that says, AMOUNT OF MONEY PEOPLE SAVED THIS YEAR BY SWITCHING FROM AT&T TO MCI, followed by a counter showing billions of dollars. After the Los Angeles earthquake the electricity failure reset the counter, so it read "$0" for a few days.

L.A.-area residents maintain their sense of humor. When East Coast people claim Los Angeles doesn't have any seasons, Los Angelenos recite the list: fire, flood, earthquake, and riot.

A minor earthquake of magnitude 4.7 in the San Francisco Bay area injured one man. He thought someone was trying to break in, so he grabbed his gun, put it in his pocket, and accidentally shot himself as he was running upstairs. Police later discovered the gun had been stolen.

This grammatically confusing notice was posted after a California earthquake: DRINKING WATER FROM TANKERS AND PORTABLE TOILETS PROVIDED IN AFFECTED AREAS. It's hard to imagine being *that* thirsty!

After the World Series Quake in 1989 some people started calling Candlestick Park "Wiggley Field." Maybe the same people were the ones claiming Barney Rubble had been elected mayor.

After an earthquake in the '70s the main street of La Crescenta, California, seemed to be littered with dead bodies. But upon a closer look they were mannequins that had been thrown through shattered store windows.

✺   ✺   ✺   ✺   ✺   ✺

San Francisco babies weren't willing to wait to be born just because there had been an earthquake. A 1906 journal records eighteen births, including one set of triplets, on a single day in park refugee camps. Certainly no one ever forgot *these* babies' birthday!

Sometimes one day can change a life forever

American Diaries

**Different girls,
living in different periods of America's past,
reveal their hearts' secrets in the pages
of their diaries. Each faces a challenge
that will change her life forever.**